D0017348

Understanding the
ANOINTING

By Kenneth E. Hagin

Unless otherwise indicated, all Scripture quotations in this volume are from the *King James Version* of the Bible.

First Printing 1983

ISBN 0-89276-507-0

In the U.S. write:
Kenneth Hagin Ministries
P.O. Box 50126
Tulsa, Oklahoma 74150

In Canada write:
Kenneth Hagin Ministries
P.O. Box 335
Islington (Toronto), Ontario
Canada, M9A 4X3

Copyright © 1983 RHEMA Bible Church
AKA Kenneth Hagin Ministries, Inc.
All Rights Reserved
Printed in USA

BOOKS BY KENNETH E. HAGIN

*Redeemed From Poverty, Sickness and Death
*What Faith Is
*Seven Vital Steps To Receiving the Holy Spirit
*Right and Wrong Thinking
 Prayer Secrets
*Authority of the Believer
*How To Turn Your Faith Loose
 The Key to Scriptural Healing
 The Ministry of a Prophet
 The Origin and Operation of Demons
 Demons and How To Deal With Them
 Ministering to the Oppressed
 Praying To Get Results
 The Present-Day Ministry of Jesus Christ
 The Gift of Prophecy
 Healing Belongs to Us
 The Real Faith
 The Interceding Christian
 How You Can Know the Will of God
 Man on Three Dimensions
 The Human Spirit
 Turning Hopeless Situations Around
 Casting Your Cares Upon the Lord
 Seven Steps for Judging Prophecy
 Faith Food for Autumn
 Faith Food for Winter
 Faith Food for Spring
 Faith Food for Summer
*The New Birth
*Why Tongues?
*In Him
*God's Medicine
*You Can Have What You Say
 How To Write Your Own Ticket With God
*Don't Blame God
*Words
 Plead Your Case
*How To Keep Your Healing
 Laying on of Hands
 A Better Covenant
 Having Faith in Your Faith
 Five Hindrances to Growth in Grace
 Why Do People Fall Under the Power?
 The Bible Way To Receive the Holy Spirit
 Godliness Is Profitable
 I Went to Hell
 Three Big Words

Obedience in Finances
His Name Shall Be Called Wonderful
I Believe in Visions
New Thresholds of Faith
Prevailing Prayer to Peace
Concerning Spiritual Gifts
Bible Faith Study Course
Bible Prayer Study Course
The Holy Spirit and His Gifts
*The Ministry Gifts (Study Guide)
Seven Things You Should Know About Divine Healing
El Shaddai
Zoe: The God-Kind of Life
A Commonsense Guide to Fasting
Must Christians Suffer?
The Woman Question
How You Can Be Led by the Spirit of God
What To Do When Faith Seems Weak and Victory Lost
The Name of Jesus
The Art of Intercession
Growing Up, Spiritually
Bodily Healing and the Atonement
Exceedingly Growing Faith
Understanding the Anointing

BOOKS BY KENNETH HAGIN JR.

Man's Impossibility — God's Possibility
Because of Jesus
The Key to the Supernatural
*Faith Worketh by Love
Blueprint for Building Strong Faith
*Seven Hindrances to Healing
*The Past Tense of God's Word
Healing: A Forever-Settled Subject
How To Make the Dream God Gave You Come True
Faith Takes Back What the Devil's Stolen
"The Prison Door Is Open — What Are You Still Doing Inside?"
Itching Ears
Where Do We Go From Here?
How To Be a Success in Life
Get Acquainted With God
Showdown With the Devil

*These titles are also available in Spanish. Information about other foreign translations of several of the above titles (i.e., Dutch, Finnish, French, German, Indonesian, Polish, Russian, Swahili, and Swedish) may be obtained by writing to: Kenneth Hagin Ministries, P.O. Box 50126, Tulsa, Oklahoma 74150.

Contents

Foreword

When I started out in the ministry 49 years ago, I wish we'd had the material that's available today. Our ministries and lives would have been different.

That's the reason I want to share with other ministers — especially young ministers — what it took some of us 40 or 50 years to learn.

In this book I want to discuss what I have learned about the anointing during my half century of ministry. There is much about it in my spirit to share with you.

In Section 1, we will discuss *the individual anointing* that all believers have in the New Birth. We will point out that all believers can experience a deeper anointing by being baptized with the Holy Spirit. This experience, open to all believers, is for service.

In Section 2 we will see that there also is an anointing of the Holy Spirit upon *ministry gifts* — an anointing that goes with the offices.

Thank God for the ministry gifts He has placed in the Body of Christ so we may grow. Thank God for the anointing of God upon men and women He's called to these offices.

There is an even stronger anointing, *the corporate anointing,* that rests upon the Church. We will study this anointing in Section 3.

Bear in mind as you read this material that these are different anointings, but they are all from the same Holy Spirit — the only member of the Godhead who is at work in the earth today.

You will find that there's nothing like the glory of God in manifestation. Once you get a taste of it, nothing else will satisfy.

Kenneth E. Hagin

Tulsa, Oklahoma
July 1983

SECTION I
The Individual Anointing

Chapter 1
The Anointing on Jesus

In Old Testament times, the common layman (we'd call him a "believer" today) had no anointing *in* him or *on* him. The presence of God was kept shut up in the Holy of Holies in the Temple.

But God would anoint the *king* to stand in that office; He would anoint the *priest* to stand in that office; and He would anoint the *prophet* to stand in that office. The Spirit of God would come *upon* these three types of individuals to enable them to stand in their respective offices.

David had all of these anointings. David was king, and he also was priest and prophet. In the 92nd Psalm, David said, "*...I shall be anointed with fresh oil*" (v. 10). Oil is a type of the Holy Spirit. (Often we need a fresh anointing.)

Anointings Today

God is still anointing *prophets* today. Prophets are spokesmen for Him. The prophetic office includes anything that speaks for God — which would be all of the teaching and preaching offices — but especially that of the prophet, because that is the anointing involved. God is still anointing people to preach, to testify, and to sing.

And He's still anointing *priests*. What was the function of the priest? He represented other people. Other people couldn't go into the presence of God in the Holy of Holies, but the priest — the High Priest — could go into the Holy of Holies, so he was the *intercessor* for the people. God is still anointing intercessors. He's anointing people to pray. There's an anointing there.

And He's anointing *kings*. We're all kings, glory to

God. Romans 5:17 says that we shall "reign in life." It's because of the anointing that we're able to reign.

Other Old Testament references to the anointing include these texts from Zechariah and Isaiah.

ZECHARIAH 4:6
6 Then he answered and spake unto me, saying, This is the word of the Lord unto Zerubbabel, saying, Not by might [or army], nor by power, but BY MY SPIRIT, saith the Lord of hosts.

We always think of might and power in connection with the Spirit of God. When God speaks of might and power in this Scripture, He's talking about human might. He's telling Zerubbabel, "It's not by the power of an army, but it's by my Spirit that the battle is going to be won." It's by the Spirit of God that victories come, not by the hand of man.

ISAIAH 10:27
27 And it shall come to pass in that day, that his burden shall be taken away from off thy shoulder, and his yoke from off thy neck, and the yoke shall be destroyed BECAUSE OF THE ANOINTING.

Sometimes we turn that phrase around and say, "It's the anointing that destroys (or breaks) the yoke." That's saying absolutely the same thing: *The yoke shall be destroyed because of the anointing.*

This is true in our lives and ministries as well: The yoke of sickness or anything else that the devil tries to put on us will be destroyed *because of the anointing.*

In the New Testament, we see how the anointing was on the ministry of Jesus, and we can learn about ministering under the anointing.

> LUKE 4:14-19
> 14 And Jesus returned in the POWER of the SPIRIT into Galilee: and there went out a fame of him through all the region round about.
> 15 And he taught in their synagogues, being glorified of all.

Notice in the fourteenth verse, the word "power" is used in connection with the Holy Spirit. Combining these two verses, we could say, "He returned in the power of the Spirit and He taught," or, "He taught in the power of the Spirit" (for there is an anointing to teach).

> 16 And he came to Nazareth, where he had been brought up: and, as his custom was, he went into the synagogue on the sabbath day, and stood up for to read.
> 17 And there was delivered unto him the book of the prophet Esaias [Isaiah]. And when he had opened the book, he found the place where it was written,
> 18 The Spirit of the Lord is upon me, because he hath ANOINTED me TO PREACH the gospel to the poor; he hath sent me TO HEAL the brokenhearted, to preach deliverance to the captives, and recovering of sight to the blind, to set at liberty them that are bruised,
> 19 To preach the acceptable year of the Lord.

Notice in connection with the Holy Spirit there first was the word "power" (v. 14) and then the word "anointed" (v. 18).

Peter, preaching to Cornelius and his household, said, *"How God ANOINTED Jesus of Nazareth with the Holy Ghost and with power: who went about doing good, and healing all that were oppressed of the devil; for God was with him"* (Acts 10:38).

Jesus said, *"The Spirit of the Lord is UPON me, because HE HATH ANOINTED ME...."* (Luke 4:18). God anointed Jesus primarily to do two things according to this entire verse: to preach and to heal. (In connection with preaching, Jesus also was anointed to teach.)

The Ministry of Jesus Christ

When you discuss the earthly ministry of the Lord Jesus Christ, most people immediately respond, "Well, yes, but He was the Son of God." And, of course, He was.

But what they fail to realize is that *He as the Son of God was one thing and He as a person ministering was another thing. He did not minister as the Son of God — He ministered as a mere man anointed by the Holy Spirit.*

If people would just stop and think for a moment, they would see this in the passage of Scripture we have just been studying in Luke 4.

He was in His hometown of Nazareth on the sabbath day, went to the synagogue, and was given the scroll of Isaiah to read from. He read the passage we just studied: *"The Spirit of the Lord is upon me, because he hath anointed me...."* After He had finished reading, Jesus handed the scroll back to the minister, sat down, and began to teach the people.

He said, *"THIS DAY is this scripture fulfilled in your ears"* (v. 21).

If Jesus had been ministering *as the Son of God,* He wouldn't have needed to be anointed. Or, if He had been ministering *as God manifested in the flesh,* would God have needed to be anointed?

Who is going to anoint God?

In Philippians 2:7, it says that Jesus *"made himself of no reputation, and took upon him the form of a servant, and was made in the likeness of men."* *The King James Version* is a little unclear here. Other translations say He "laid aside" or "stripped Himself" of "His mighty power and glory" when He came into this world, even though He was the Son of God.

He came as a man. How did He do it? I don't know. The Bible says He did it, and I believe it!

As I've said many times, Jesus was just as much the Son of God when He was 21 years old as He was when He was 30 years old. He was just as much the Son of God when He was 25 as He was when He was 30. He was just as much the Son of God all those years — 25, 26, 27, 28, 29, wasn't He? Yet in all of those years, He never healed a person or wrought a miracle!

How do we know this? Because the Bible says so. The Bible tells us that Jesus was anointed after He was baptized of John in Jordan, and the Holy Spirit came upon Him in a bodily shape like a dove (Luke 3:22). God spoke from heaven and said, *"This is my beloved Son, in whom I am well pleased"* (Matt. 3:17).

Jesus' First Miracle

Then the Word of God tells us about Jesus' returning into the Galilee and attending the wedding feast at Cana with His mother. There He turned water into wine, and the Bible says this was the first miracle Jesus wrought: *"This beginning of miracles did Jesus in Cana of Galilee, and manifested forth his glory; and his disciples believed on him"* (John 2:11).

Jesus also had to be anointed before He could heal, because He had laid aside His mighty power and glory as the Son of God when He became a man. Although in person He was the Son of God, in power He was not the Son of God. Even though this may sound like a paradox, can you understand it?

When people say, "Well, yes — but Jesus was the Son of God," that puts Him *in ministry* in a class by Himself. That would mean that *nobody else could minister that way* — or even come close to it — if Jesus in ministry is in a class by Himself.

Now, *as a person*, because He is the Son of God, He *is* in a class by Himself. But *in ministry*, He is *not* in a class by Himself.

Why? Remember what Jesus said in John's Gospel?

> **JOHN 14:12**
> 12 Verily, verily, I say unto you, He that believeth on me, the works that I do shall he do also; and GREATER WORKS THAN THESE SHALL HE DO; because I go unto my Father.

Therefore, if Jesus' works — His ministry is His works — were in a class by themselves, as so many people believe, then Jesus told a falsehood. He said, "...*the works that I do shall he* [who believes on Jesus] *do also; and GREATER WORKS than these shall he do....*"

So Jesus Himself did not place His works or His ministry in a class by themselves.

Why has this not been properly understood? We have not thoroughly studied the Word on this subject because we have been religiously brainwashed. We have thought,

*Well, there's no need of going into that, because Jesus is
the Son of God, and I couldn't minister that way, anyway.*
And so, of course, we've missed it.

Jesus in the Fivefold Ministries

Paul wrote in Ephesians 4:8 that when Christ ascended
on High, He gave gifts to men. What were these gifts?
They are listed in the eleventh verse: *"And he gave some,
APOSTLES; and some, PROPHETS; and some, EVAN-
GELISTS; and some, PASTORS and TEACHERS...."*
These are commonly referred to as "the fivefold ministry
gifts."

Actually, Jesus stood in all of the fivefold ministries
— every one of them — and He's our example in every one
of them.

First, He stood in the office of the *apostle.* He's called
an apostle in the third chapter of Hebrews:

> **HEBREWS 3:1**
> 1 Wherefore, holy brethren, partakers of the heavenly
> calling, consider the APOSTLE and High Priest of our
> profession, Christ Jesus.

The Greek word *apostolos* translated "apostle" means
"a sent one," so Jesus is the foremost example of "a sent
one." He was sent by God and by the Holy Spirit.

Second, Jesus stood in the office of the *prophet.* Jesus
calls Himself a prophet in the fourth chapter of Luke's
Gospel: *"No PROPHET is accepted in his own country"*
(v. 24).

Then you remember the story of the woman at the well
in Samaria. She said she wanted the living water Jesus

promised, but when He told her to go get her husband, she admitted, "*I have no husband*" (John 4:17).

Jesus replied, "*Thou hast well said, I have no husband: For thou hast had five husbands; and he whom thou now hast is not thy husband: in that saidst thou truly*" (vv. 17,18).

In other words, Jesus said the man she was living with wasn't her husband. (In this modern day, we've encountered some people even in charismatic circles who are living together without marriage, saying, "Oh well, God knows, and he's really my husband." He's no more your husband than you are a monkey's uncle.)

The woman at Jacob's Well acknowledged, "*Sir, I perceive that thou art a PROPHET*" (v. 19). She left her waterpot, returned to the city, and told the people, "*Come, see a man, which told me all things that ever I did: is not this the Christ?*" (v. 29).

One aspect of the prophet's ministry is that he sees and knows things supernaturally. (In the Old Testament he sometimes was called a "seer.") So Jesus was a prophet.

He also stood in the office of the *evangelist.* He said in Luke 4:18, "*The Spirit of the Lord is upon me, because he hath anointed me to PREACH THE GOSPEL . . . .*" That's what the evangelist is anointed to do: preach the Gospel, the Good News.

Fourth, Jesus stood in the office of *pastor.* He said, "*I am the good SHEPHERD*" (John 10:14). The word "shepherd" is the same word that's translated "pastor." Peter calls Jesus "*the chief Shepherd*" (1 Peter 5:4).

Fifth, Jesus stood in the office of *teacher.* The four Gospels say more about His teaching than anything else, if you go through and underline the word "teach" or "taught." Jesus taught more than He healed. He taught more than He preached. Teaching was first with Him.

Matthew 9:35 says, *"He went about all the cities and villages, TEACHING in their synagogues, and PREACH-ING the gospel of the kingdom, and HEALING every sickness and every disease among the people."*

His ministry consisted of *teaching, preaching,* and *healing.* There is an anointing that goes with each of these offices.

And if you'll function in your office, the anointing will be there. It can become stronger — it can be increased — or you can cause it to diminish and decrease, as we will study later.

The Spirit Without Measure

John the Baptist, speaking about Jesus, infers Jesus had the Holy Spirit *without measure,* inferring that we as individuals have the Spirit *by measure:*

JOHN 3:34
34 For he whom God hath sent speaketh the words of God: for God giveth NOT the Spirit BY MEASURE unto him.

There is a measure of the Holy Spirit *in* the believer for a certain purpose, but an anointing *comes upon* you to stand in the office (or ministry) to which God has called you. Although it's the same Holy Spirit, it's a different anointing.

Because the Lord Jesus Christ had the Holy Spirit without measure, He stood in all five of the main ministry gifts, and He is the model for all of us to follow.

Chapter 2
The Anointing Within

Now he which stablisheth us with you in Christ, and hath ANOINTED us, is God;
Who hath also sealed us, and given the earnest of the Spirit in our hearts.

2 Corinthians 1:21,22

But ye have an UNCTION from the Holy One, and ye know all things . . . .
But the ANOINTING which ye have received of him abideth IN you, and ye need not that any man teach you: but as the same ANOINTING teacheth you of all things, and is truth, and is no lie, and even as it hath taught you, ye shall abide in him.

1 John 2:20,27

In these two verses from First John, the terms "unction" and "anointing" are used. The Greek word is the same in both verses.

Every believer has an anointing — an unction — that abides within him, because the Holy Spirit comes in us in the New Birth. Romans 8:9 says, *"Now if any man have not the Spirit of Christ, he is none of his."* The Spirit of Christ is the Holy Spirit.

We're not referring here to being baptized with the Holy Spirit, or being filled with the Holy Spirit, as the Bible terms it. That is a separate experience from the New Birth.

Two Spiritual Experiences

There is a dual working of the Spirit of God in the life

of a believer: the New Birth and the baptism in the Holy Spirit.

In His teaching to the woman at the well of Samaria, Jesus said, "*. . .the water that I shall give him shall be IN him a well of water springing up into everlasting life*" (John 4:14).

In the seventh chapter of John's Gospel, Jesus said, "*He that believeth on me, as the scripture hath said, OUT of his belly shall flow rivers of living water*" (v. 38).

Jesus told His disciples, "*And I will pray the Father, and he shall give you another Comforter, that he may abide with you for ever; Even the Spirit of truth . . . for he dwelleth WITH you, and shall be IN you*" (John 14:16,17).

Later, Jesus told the disciples, "*But ye shall receive power AFTER that the Holy Ghost is come UPON you: and ye shall be witnesses unto me. . . .*" (Acts 1:8).

It's obvious that these are two different experiences Jesus is talking about. One — the New Birth — *blesses you.* It's water IN YOU springing up into everlasting life.

The other experience — the baptism in the Holy Spirit — *makes you a blessing to others.* It is those rivers flowing OUT of you; it is the enduement of power Jesus promised in Luke 24 — and it is available to every believer.

LUKE 24:49
49 And, behold, I send the promise of my Father upon you: but tarry ye in the city of Jerusalem, until ye be endued with power from on high.

Life in the Spirit

In studying the Holy Spirit in the life of the believer who has been born of the Spirit and baptized with the Holy Spirit, we see many things.

We find that the Holy Spirit in us *bears witness* with our spirit that we are the children of God (Rom. 8:16).

We find that *"as many as are led by the Spirit of God, they are the sons of God"* (Rom. 8:14).

We also find it is the Holy Spirit who *quickens: "If the Spirit of him that raised up Jesus from the dead dwell in you, he that raised up Christ from the dead shall also quicken* [or make full of life] *your mortal bodies* [your death-doomed bodies] *by his Spirit that dwelleth in you"* (Rom. 8:11).

We find how the Holy Spirit *helps us pray.* For example, in First Corinthians 14:14, Paul said, *"For if I pray in an unknown tongue, my spirit prayeth...."*

Or, as *The Amplified Bible* has it: "For if I pray in an [unknown] tongue, my spirit [by the Holy Spirit within me] prays, but my mind is unproductive — bears no fruit and helps nobody. Then what am I to do? I will pray with my spirit — by the Holy Spirit that is within me; but I will also pray intelligently — with my mind and understanding; I will sing with my spirit — by the Holy Spirit that is within me; but I will sing (intelligently) with my mind and understanding also" (vv. 14,15).

Then we read in Romans 8:26,27: *"Likewise the Spirit also helpeth our infirmities* [or weaknesses]: *for we know not what we should pray for as we ought...."* One of our weaknesses is that we know not for what to pray as we ought!

"...But the Spirit itself maketh intercession for us with groanings which cannot be uttered. And he that searcheth the hearts knoweth what is the mind of the Spirit, because he maketh intercession for the saints according to the will of God."

By putting these verses together, we can see that in groanings and in praying with other tongues, it's the Spirit helping us pray for things we don't know how to pray for as we should. But, thank God, He knows. Thank God for the Holy Spirit in the life of the believer!

Let's look again at what Jesus said to the disciples about the Holy Spirit in the fourteenth chapter of John:

> **JOHN 14:16,17**
> **16 And I will pray the Father, and he shall give you another Comforter, that he may abide with you for ever;**
> **17 Even the Spirit of truth; whom the world cannot receive, because it seeth him not, neither knoweth him: but ye know him; for he dwelleth WITH you, and SHALL BE IN YOU.**

Many translations read, "I'll not leave you helpless. I'll send you another Helper." The Greek word *parakletos* that's translated "Comforter" here means "one called alongside to help."

The Amplified translation brings out the sevenfold meaning of the Greek word in this sixteenth verse: It means *Comforter, Counselor, Helper, Intercessor, Advocate, Strengthener,* and *Standby* — and He's all of these.

The Holy Spirit as Teacher

In addition to helping us *pray* and *witness,* that anointing helps us by *teaching* us.

In verse 17, Jesus called the Comforter the Spirit of truth. He said in John 15:26, *"But when the Comforter is come, whom I will send unto you from the Father, even the Spirit of truth, which proceedeth from the Father, he shall testify of me."*

The Holy Spirit never testifies of Himself. He testifies of Jesus.

Jesus speaks to us by the Holy Spirit. Jesus is not here on earth today with a flesh-and-blood body, because His body was resurrected, and it's now *flesh and bone* (Luke 24:39), the *blood* having been shed for our sins. With a flesh-and-bone body, Jesus is seated at the right hand of God (Rom. 8:34) and "ever liveth to make intercession" for us (Heb. 7:25).

So He's not here in the natural, but, thank God, the Holy Spirit is, and Jesus speaks to us by the Spirit. *When the anointing teaches you, that's Jesus teaching you,* because He said, *"I will pray the Father, and he shall give you another Comforter, that he may abide with you for ever"* (John 14:16); and when He — the Comforter, the Helper, the *Paraclete* — has come, *"he will guide you into all truth . . . ."* (John 16:13). Thank God He does.

This verse continues, *". . .for he shall not speak of himself; but whatsoever he shall hear, that shall he speak: and he will shew you things to come."*

Jesus said more in the 15th verse: *". . .he shall take of mine, and shall shew it unto you."*

So these are other works of the Holy Spirit: to guide us into all truth; to take the things of Jesus and show them to us; and, in John 14:

JOHN 14:26
26 But the Comforter, which is the Holy Ghost, whom the Father will send in my name, he shall teach you all things, and bring all things to your remembrance, whatsoever I have said unto you.

Did you ever notice how the Holy Spirit will bring to

your remembrance Scriptures that you hardly knew —
maybe you read them once? Praise God, that's His work
in the believer.

John, writing in his first epistle, First John 2:20, calls
this anointing "an unction."

> **1 JOHN 2:20**
> 20 But ye have an UNCTION from the Holy One, and ye
> know all things.

The Spirit of Revelation

The Holy Spirit is supposed to show you all things. In
First Corinthians, Paul talks about the fact that *"Eye hath
not seen, nor ear heard, neither have entered into the heart
of man, the things which God hath prepared for them that
love him"* (1 Cor. 2:9).

Often we read that verse — I guess we've all been guilty
of it sometime or other — and said, "Now isn't that
wonderful? He's going to provide things we've never seen
and don't know about." But that's not what God's talking about at all. The very next verse says, *"But God
HATH revealed them unto us by His Spirit: for the Spirit
searcheth all things, yea, the deep things of God"* (v. 10).

Hallelujah! The Holy Spirit is a Spirit of revelation.
He'll *"take of mine, and shall shew it unto you."*

John said, "You've received an unction, and you know
all things." *The reason we don't know more than we know
is because we haven't listened to that Teacher* — the Holy
Spirit is a Teacher.

Then in the 27th verse of First John 2, John writes,
*"But the ANOINTING which ye have received of him
ABIDETH IN YOU, and ye need not that any man teach*

you: but as the same ANOINTING teacheth you of all things, and is truth, and is no lie, and even as it hath taught you, ye shall abide in him. "

Notice that the anointing which you've received of Him abideth *in you.* Where is the anointing? IN YOU. Doesn't that sound like what Jesus said in John 14:17?

> **JOHN 14:17**
> 17 Even the Spirit of truth; whom the world cannot receive, because it seeth him not, neither knoweth him: but ye know him; for he dwelleth with you, and shall be IN YOU.

He shall be where? IN YOU. Automatically we think of First John 4:4: "*...greater is he that is IN YOU....*" Here John calls that anointing "he," because He is a divine personality. *"Greater is he that is in you, than he that is in the world."* I doubt seriously if any of us have ever taken advantage of Him who dwells in us, living in the fullness of what that means. If this is the case — if He dwells in us — then immediately we *don't have to be afraid of anything that's in this world, because we have Someone in us who's bigger than anything in the world!*

"Yes," people complain, "but you don't know what I've got to put up with!"

I don't care what you've got to put up with. He's bigger! He's greater!

In First John 2:27 we saw the phrase, *"ye need not that any man teach you."* That doesn't mean that God hasn't set teachers in the Church! That doesn't mean we don't need teachers! The Holy Spirit will not contradict Himself.

Did you ever stop to think that when a man teaches under the inspiration of the Holy Spirit, it is not *man* teaching us something — it's *the Holy Spirit* teaching us?

The Holy Spirit will teach us, and when we hear the Word taught, the Holy Spirit also will bear witness with our spirit if the teaching is right.

Beyond the Bible

A certain teacher caused a lot of trouble once for a friend of mine, a man who had been a Bible teacher for 35 years. My friend had taken his Bible class to this man's meetings, but found his teaching began to be increasingly in error.

Finally he handed the man his Bible, saying, "You're going to have to give me chapter and verse for that. You're going to have to show that to me in the Bible."

The traveling teacher handed the Bible back to him, saying, "Oh, you won't find what I'm preaching in *that thing*." (When you start calling the Bible "that thing," you're in trouble.)

"Oh, no," he said, "I'm way out beyond that thing."

If you've gotten out *beyond* the Bible, you've gotten out beyond the Holy Spirit, because the Bible says that the Spirit and the Word are one [agree], as John states in First John 5:7.

What was amazing to me was that my friend, a man who was saved, baptized in the Holy Spirit, and a Bible teacher in a Full Gospel church, got taken in by this false teacher and lost half his class!

On the other hand, a young Chinese woman, who had been converted only two weeks earlier in a tent meeting, went to the same teacher's meetings one night but realized he was in error. She told me, "You know, something on the inside of me told me, 'Don't go back.' So we never went back."

She was just a baby Christian — she didn't even have the baptism in the Holy Spirit yet — but she listened to the Spirit who was *in* her.

I think what happens to us is we go by our heads instead of our spirits after we have been Christians for many years. Often our heads have been educated at the expense of our spirits.

The Spirit of God will teach us. That's what the Spirit of God was teaching the Chinese woman: "That's not right. Don't go there."

Of course God put teachers in the Church — teaching is one of the fivefold ministries, and that's one way God teaches us. On the other hand, the Teacher is also in us. He'll let us know when it's right and He'll let us know when it's not right. And *every believer has that anointing in him or her.* We don't need to pray for it. We've got it.

Why Christians Are Defeated

Oh, how real He is! If people would start developing that consciousness of the indwelling Spirit when they first become Christians, He would manifest Himself. But too often they haven't been taught correctly.

They thought they got an "experience." They kept trying to have another experience like that one, but it wasn't an experience at all; it was Someone — a divine Personality — who came to live in them. He is a heavenly Being: the Holy Spirit.

So often we have been defeated because we weren't taught this — or we were taught something that isn't so, and we have had to "unlearn" it. It's a lot harder to "unlearn" than it is to learn. Before we can walk on with

God, sometimes we've got to "unlearn" some things.

We must learn to look to our (human) spirit, even when our mind can't grasp what we're hearing. I've heard men preach, I've listened to tapes, and I've studied books — and my head just couldn't grasp it. But on the inside of me, it felt like something was turning flips. I knew my spirit, because of the Holy Spirit within me, was telling me, "That's so." But even with this witness, I've had problems accepting these things. Have you ever had such problems, or am I the only one?

What we think, or the way we've been taught often hinders us from moving into the Spirit realm. It also will keep us from praying in tongues.

Paul said, *"For if I pray in an unknown tongue, my spirit prayeth, but my understanding is unfruitful"* (1 Cor. 14:14). Our understanding, or, we might say, our mind — it would be the same thing — wants to get in on everything, but it can't get in on praying in the Spirit unless God gives the interpretation.

Therefore, our mind will try to talk us out of praying in tongues. Even after we've prayed a while, our mind will say, "Well, what good did that do?"

Then, of course, the devil will side in with that unrenewed mind, agreeing, "What good did you get out of that? You don't know one word you said! Isn't that foolish? Anyway, that didn't sound much like a language."

That's our problem: We pass judgment on something instead of listening to what God's Word says about it. God even said in Isaiah 28:11, *"With stammering lips and another tongue will he [God] speak unto this people."* So, bless God, if you just stammered, that's the Holy Spirit, too! Accept it and go on with God. Expect more, and He'll give you more.

The Temple of God

We saw earlier the text from First John 4:4: "...*greater is he that is IN YOU, than he that is in the world.*" Here John is talking about the Holy Spirit who is in us — "*Christ IN YOU, the hope of glory*" (Col. 1:27). He dwells in us by the power of the Spirit.

In First Corinthians 3, Paul uses different terms to say the same thing John said. John said, "...*the anointing which ye have received of him abideth IN YOU....*" (1 John 2:20). Here Paul is saying, "*Know ye not that ye are the temple of God, and that the Spirit of God dwelleth IN YOU?*" (1 Cor. 3:16).

Look at First Corinthians 6:19: "*What? know ye not that your body is the temple of the Holy Ghost which is in you, which ye have of God, and ye are not your own?*"

Then notice this second letter Paul wrote to the Corinthians. He must have wanted to reemphasize this truth:

> 2 CORINTHIANS 6:14-16
> 14 Be ye not unequally yoked together with unbelievers: for what fellowship hath righteousness with unrighteousness? and what communion hath light with darkness?
> 15 And what concord hath Christ with Belial? or what part hath he that believeth with an infidel?
> 16 And what agreement hath the temple of God with idols? for ye are the temple of the living God; as God hath said, I will dwell IN them, and walk IN them; and I will be their God, and they shall be my people.

The believer is called a "believer," and the unbeliever is called an "unbeliever."

The believer is called "righteousness," and the unbeliever is called "unrighteousness."

The believer is called "light," and the unbeliever is called "darkness."

The believer is called "Christ," and the unbeliever is called "Belial."

The believer is called "the temple of God," and the unbeliever is called "idols."

That's shouting ground, isn't it? *"Ye are the temple of the living God; as God hath said, I will dwell in them* [live in them, in other words] *and walk in them . . . ."*

So there is an individual (or personal) anointing of the Holy Spirit that abides IN each one of us. We need to learn to take advantage of it.

Chapter 3
How the Anointing Led Me

The text we just studied from First John says, *"the anointing which ye have received of him abideth IN you . . .* [and] *teacheth you of all things."* What is that anointing for? It's to teach you all things!

I remember the night I was born again: I was born again the 22nd day of April 1933. I know that an unction or anointing came into me that very night. I am just as conscious of it on the *inside* of me as I am of my two ears on the *outside* of me.

The Holy Spirit began to try to teach me a lot of things, but my head wouldn't go along with it. I didn't know to listen to Him. So often we have been religiously brainwashed. Our heads are all cluttered up with religious things, and we have not been trained to listen to and follow our spirits.

But it was there on that bed of sickness as a 15- and 16-year-old invalid that I got into the Word, and the Spirit of God taught me about divine healing.

Five doctors had told me, "You're going to die — that's all there is to it. You can't live. There's not one chance in a million for you to live."

But something inside me — that anointing that teaches you all things — that inward "something" — said, "You don't have to die. Not now. Not at this age. Not as a teenager. You can live. You can be healed!"

I said, "Can I?"

Something inside me said, "It's all in the Book. Get in the Book. The Bible — that's where it is!" And thank God I got in there, and He taught me. I didn't have an

23

earthly teacher.

It was difficult, however. It's easier to learn spiritual things if you have a human teacher, because you can see the teacher, listen to him or her, and the witness of the Holy Spirit on the inside of you will let you know whether or not they're teaching what is right.

Thank God, He taught me. I listened to Him, and He led me right into the Word, right into faith — and right into healing.

What if I never had listened? I never would have been taught; I would have died and gone on to glory and missed doing what God called me to do; and we wouldn't have any RHEMA Bible Training Center. I'm so glad I learned to listen!

I saw after my healing that if I had listened to what that "something" on the inside of me had been trying to tell me, I would have been out of that bed a lot sooner. I was an invalid 16 long months before I was healed.

I'll challenge anybody anywhere that if they've got the Holy Spirit living inside them — the One who is the Author of the Bible — He'll lead them right into divine healing. If it's the same Holy Spirit who authored this Book, He's going to teach you what's in there.

When He opened the Word to me, I acted upon the Word. I didn't know anybody who believed in divine healing, so I didn't have anybody to pray for me. I learned to listen, thank God, to my spirit.

On the inside of me was this voice teaching me. It said, "You believe all right as far as you know, but that last clause of Mark 11:24 — *"and ye shall have them"* — goes with the preceding clause, *"believe that ye receive them."*

MARK 11:24
24 Therefore I say unto you, What things soever ye desire, when ye pray, believe that ye receive them, and ye shall have them.

Like a flash, I saw it. What I'd been trying to do was get healed first — have it first — and *then* I was going to believe it. He said, *"Believe it first,* and then you'll have it."

So I began to say, right out loud in my room, "I believe. I believe. I believe I receive healing for the deformed heart. I believe I receive healing for the paralysis. I believe I receive healing for the incurable blood disease."

And while I was saying that and praising God for it, that anointing in me — IN me — said, "Arise. People who are well ought to be up at 10:30 in the morning."

I thought for a moment, *How am I going to get up? I'm paralyzed.* But when I made the effort and acted upon the Word, the power of God came down on me and went through me like a bolt of electricity!

I stood upright on my feet and was healed — and I have been healed ever since. I say this to the glory of God: I've had half a century of divine health.

The last headache I had was in August 1933, but don't misunderstand me: I'm not opposed to doctors. Thank God for them. Medical science will help people as much as it can. If I'd have needed to go to a doctor in the past half century, I would have gone — but I haven't needed to. I've sent other people to the doctor, however, paid their bills, and bought their medicine. (Doctors often can keep people alive until we can get enough Word in them to get them healed.)

My healing came about by my listening to that inward

anointing that teaches you all things. I listened, obeyed, and off the bed I came.

I would challenge anybody who is born again (because you're born of the Holy Spirit): The Spirit will lead you into the baptism of the Holy Spirit. It was that same Spirit — that same anointing that teaches — who led me into the baptism of the Holy Spirit.

After my healing, I began to seek out the fellowship of those who believed like I did.

Some Full Gospel people had come to our town. Even though there were a lot of things about them that I didn't understand and didn't agree with, I didn't criticize them. I welcomed them with open arms. I was glad to find somebody who believed in faith and healing that I could fellowship with. We need fellowship.

Now, you don't have to go to Full Gospel services too long until people start preaching and testifying about the baptism in the Holy Spirit and speaking in tongues. When they did, I closed my ears, because I didn't know whether it was right or wrong. I thought, *I'll just put up with a little fanaticism to have a little fellowship around faith and healing.* I was about to enroll in a Baptist seminary.

Yes, you can be thoroughly saved, get people saved and healed every Sunday, see miracles performed, and still close your ears to other things of the Word. God will bless you all He can, because He's out to bless you. He's not out to "get" you, praise the Lord.

He'll confirm His Word. If you preach about salvation, people will get saved. If you preach about healing, people will get healed.

I preached water baptism, and people got baptized in water. I preached prayer, and people prayed. I preached living right, and people lived right. But none of them got baptized with the Holy Spirit, because I never said anything about it!

'This Holy Ghost Business'

Walking down the street one day in April 1937 in my hometown, I said to the Lord, "Now, Lord, who's right about this Holy Ghost business?

"My church says that if you're born again, you're born of the Spirit [and that's true, but a half truth does more damage than an untruth]. They say that's all there is to it; it ends right there." And I began to quote Dr. So-and-so and another renowned Baptist minister.

Then I said, "Now, these Pentecostal people say that they're baptized with the Holy Spirit according to Acts 2:4. But one or two other Baptist fellows whom I like real well tell me there is an experience subsequent to salvation called the baptism in the Holy Spirit — it is an enduement of power from on High — but you don't have to speak with tongues. I'm prone to follow them. *Who's right about this?* "

I didn't have the baptism of the Holy Spirit, but I did have Him in me, because I'm born of the Spirit and His Spirit bears witness with my spirit that I'm a child of God.

The minute I asked "Who's right?" that anointing in me began to teach me. No, there was no thundering voice on the outside; it was just that still, small voice, as we call it, that every believer has.

On the inside of me, He spoke up so plainly. He knew that I knew the Word, for I read it constantly. (Before I ever started preaching, I had read the New Testament 150 times and portions of it more than that.)

He said, "What does Acts 2:38 say?"

"Oh," I said, "Acts 2:38 says, '*Repent, and be baptized every one of you in the name of Jesus Christ for the remission of sins, and ye shall receive the gift of the Holy Ghost.*'"

That inward voice said, "What was that last statement you just said?"

I said, "'*And ye shall receive the gift of the Holy Ghost.*'"

"Well, what does the next verse say?"

I answered, "Acts 2:39 says, '*For the promise is unto you, and to your children, and to all that are afar off, even as many as the Lord our God shall call.*'"

"What promise is that?" the inward voice asked.

As I hesitated, that inward voice said, "Quote that last clause of verse 38."

I said, "'*And ye shall receive the gift of the Holy Ghost.*' Yes, Lord," I continued, "I believe that all right. I believe in the Holy Spirit now. It's those *tongues* that I don't believe in and don't know about."

And that inward voice said, "What did Acts 2:4 say?"

Very glibly, I said, "Acts 2:4 says, '*And they were all filled with the Holy Ghost, and began to . . .*' Oh, I see it. I see it! I see it! '*. . . and BEGAN TO SPEAK WITH OTHER TONGUES, as the Spirit gave them utterance.*'"

The same Spirit I was born of and became acquainted with on the bed of sickness taught me about divine healing and the baptism of the Holy Spirit. The same Spirit led me, for the unction abides in me.

Receiving the baptism of the Holy Spirit is receiving the same Spirit. It's a deeper dimension. It's entering into the fullness of what God has for us.

So walking down the street in my hometown, I immediately said, "I'm going down to the Full Gospel pastor's
house and receive the Holy Spirit right now." (That's
pretty good for a Baptist boy pastor.)

It was the custom among Full Gospel people in those
days to have tarrying services to be filled with the Holy
Spirit. I think it's fine to wait on God, but don't tarry to
be filled with the Holy Spirit. Get filled first and *then* tarry.
I think that's one place we've missed it. We ought to have
tarrying meetings — waiting meetings.

When I told the pastor, "I came down here to receive
the Holy Spirit," the first thing he said was, "Wait."

I said, "It won't take me long to receive." If you've
heard my story, you know it wasn't eight minutes until
I was talking in tongues.

I prayed, "Lord, I came down here to be filled with the
Holy Spirit. I know I have the Holy Spirit in me in the
New Birth."

I quoted to the Lord what the Scripture said in Acts
2:38. Then I said, "Lord, I received my salvation — my
New Birth — by faith. I received my healing by faith. Now
I receive this experience by faith. I want to declare by faith
that I am filled with the Holy Spirit. Glory to God, I have
it. And now I expect to speak with tongues. Hallelujah!"

We didn't say "hallelujah" in my church, but I said
it half a dozen times. It felt like somebody had built a bon-
fire inside me. It began to burn and it blazed up. It seemed
like I could "see" strange words coming up, and it seemed
like I knew what they would *sound* like if they were *spoken.*
I started speaking them out.

I talked in tongues for an hour and a half and sang

three songs in tongues, glory to God.

That anointing — the same Spirit — the same voice — that led me into divine healing of a deformed heart and almost total paralysis led me right into this experience. He'll teach you, too, if you'll listen to Him.

Every believer has that anointing.

Notice I didn't say every Spirit-filled believer. Every believer has that anointing in him.

Chapter 4
Ministering Healing
Without an Anointing

The Scripture doesn't say, "These signs shall follow those who are baptized with the Holy Spirit"; it says, "... *these signs shall follow them that BELIEVE* ... *they shall lay hands on the sick, and they shall recover*" (Mark 16:17,18).

I'd tell my Baptist congregation that. I'd preach it from the pulpit, but I didn't lay hands on them publicly. When I'd visit them in their homes, I'd read this to them.

"See, it says right here. We believe, don't we? Don't you believe on Jesus?"

"Yeah, I believe on Him, all right," they'd say.

"I'm going to lay my hands on you, and God is going to heal you," I'd tell them.

After coming into Pentecostal circles, I found from talking to the pastors that while I was a Baptist boy preacher, without the baptism of the Holy Spirit, I was getting a higher percentage of my people healed than any five Pentecostal pastors were their people. Some said they seldom got anybody healed. It was a common occurrence with me. The difference was that I was teaching faith and prayer. I didn't have any anointing; I didn't feel anything; and nothing went out of me into them.

One of these early experiences with healing involved the pianist of the little country church I was pastoring. When she wasn't there one Sunday, I asked about her and was told she was in the hospital and was scheduled for surgery the following morning.

I got up very early the next morning to get to her before

they gave her a shot and I couldn't communicate with her. The sun wasn't up yet when I arrived at the hospital.

I read the Scripture to her. I said, "I'm going to pray for you. Here's what the Bible says."

I had a little bottle of olive oil, and I told her, "I'm going to anoint you with oil." Then I said, "Here it says that these signs shall follow them that believe. They will lay hands on the sick. I'm going to lay hands on you."

Although I was used to seeing people get healed, I didn't expect it to happen as fast as it did. When I started praying for her, she exclaimed, "WHOOOO! I've got it!" and jumped right out of bed. She never was operated on. Now, if that'll work for the Baptists, it'll work for anybody! And I didn't have the baptism with the Holy Spirit yet.

I saw healings like hers as a Baptist preacher when I didn't have any *special anointing* to pray for the sick, and I never felt a thing. Being Baptist, I didn't know I was *supposed* to feel anything. Yet God honors His Word.

When I changed over into the Full Gospel ministry, I didn't get a "new" Holy Spirit, or a different Holy Spirit. He's not twins. He's not triplets. There's just one Holy Spirit — but the anointing may be varied. Actually, He does all the work of God.

My fellow ministers and Bible teachers among the Southern Baptists had warned me against going among Full Gospel people. One outstanding Bible teacher, a graduate of a famous Baptist seminary, said, "Kenneth, now you be careful about those Full Gospel people."

"Why?" I asked.

"That speaking in tongues is of the devil," he said.

I didn't know whether it was or wasn't. I just knew

the Pentecostals were right in believing about divine healing, so I kept fellowshipping with them. It strengthened
my faith to be around people who believed in healing. After
I got filled with the Holy Spirit and spoke with other
tongues, I almost ran to find that Bible teacher.

And in case he didn't bring it up, I brought up the subject myself.

He began to warn me again: "Now you want to be
careful about those Full Gospel people."

"Why?"

Before he criticized them he said, "Well now, I'll admit
they live better lives than we do, and in a lot of ways
they're very fundamental in their beliefs — *but that speaking in tongues is of the devil!*"

"Is it?" I asked.

"Yes," he said. "It is."

I asked, "Then the Spirit that gave them utterance in
tongues is the spirit of the devil?"

"That's right."

I said, "If that's so, then the whole Southern Baptist
movement is of the devil."

He nearly swallowed his Adam's apple. He eventually came up for air, sputtering, "Why — what are you talking about?"

"Well," I said, "the same Holy Spirit that I was born
of in the Baptist church — the *same* Holy Spirit — gave
me utterance in tongues, and I spoke with other tongues.
It was the same Holy Spirit — the *same* Spirit."

"Oh, no, no, no, no — don't say a thing like that!"

"Why?"

"Oh, it can't be so."

I said, "How do you know?"

"I just know."

I asked, "Have you ever spoken in tongues?"

"No."

"Well," I said, "don't be a fool, then. You're a Bible teacher. In Proverbs it says a fool answers a matter before he hears it. Don't be a fool. You've never spoken in tongues. You're not qualified to speak on the subject. Now, you know the Spirit you got in the New Birth, don't you?"

"Yeah."

"That's the *same* Spirit I got among the Baptists when I was born again. It was the *same* Holy Spirit. It was the *same* Spirit I've had all the time — I didn't get another spirit. And He is the One who gave me utterance in other tongues."

"Oh, that can't be so. I—I—I—I'll give that a little further study and then I'll get back to you."

Some 46 years have passed, and he's never gotten back to me yet.

The point is, *that unction IN you is to teach you,* and, thank God, He will.

SECTION II
Anointing on Ministry Gifts

Chapter 5
The Fivefold Ministry Gifts

The Word of God will work with or without an anointing.

But there also is an anointing that comes upon those whom God has called and separated unto the ministry. It's the same Holy Spirit, but the anointing to stand in a certain office is different from that anointing that abides within every believer. With the anointing, you're better able to teach, preach, and do more.

In the Old Testament, only the prophet, priest, and king were anointed.

We saw in Section 1 that Jesus stood in the fivefold ministry offices listed in the New Testament: (1) *apostle*, (2) *prophet*, (3) *evangelist*, (4) *pastor*, and (5) *teacher.*

The Word of God teaches that there are other ministries as well, such as helps, but the fivefold ministries seem to be the main pivotal gifts.

First Corinthians 12 and Romans 12 list the other ministry gifts. The anointing will come upon you to stand in these offices, too, if you are called to them.

1 CORINTHIANS 12:28
28 And God hath set some in the church, first APOSTLES, secondarily PROPHETS, thirdly TEACHERS, after that MIRACLES, then GIFTS OF HEALINGS, HELPS, GOVERNMENTS, DIVERSITIES OF TONGUES.

ROMANS 12:6-8
6 Having then gifts differing according to the grace that is given to us, whether PROPHECY, let us prophesy according to the proportion of faith;
7 Or MINISTRY, let us wait on our ministering: or he that TEACHETH, on teaching;

8 Or he that EXHORTETH, on exhortation: he that
GIVETH, let him do it with simplicity; he that RULETH,
with diligence; he that SHEWETH MERCY, with cheer-
fulness.

You can stand in more than one office, but you need
to find out where you are and what your office is and yield
to that. Then God will use you, and you will excel in your
calling.

God didn't call us all to do the same thing. Sometimes
we ministers try to be a jack-of-all-trades and we become
the master of none. We try to do too much, we spread
ourselves too thin, and the anointing's not there to do it.

That's the reason people get in trouble: They try to
function in an office to which God didn't call them. They
do something just because somebody else is doing it. And
that is very dangerous.

I remember something that Brother Howard Carter
said. He was a great teacher and a great man of God. I
never knew him personally, but I had an opportunity to
hear him preach once in Texas. After the service, I met
him. He was about 70 at the time, and he lived to be
over 80.

While we were talking, a woman came up to him,
asking, "Brother Carter, would you pray for the healing
of my child?"

He answered, "Go get my wife to lay hands on her. God
doesn't use me much along that line, but nearly everybody
she lays hands on gets healed, and nearly everybody I lay
hands on gets baptized with the Holy Spirit." (That's a
good combination, isn't it?)

I'd seen him take 19 people into a side room that night,

speak a few words to them, lay hands on them, and all 19 of them began to speak in tongues the minute he touched them.

He said, "That's my ministry. That's where my anointing is. My wife's anointing is to lay hands on the sick."

When the woman left to look for Sister Carter, Brother Carter turned to us preachers and said, "Of course, I could have prayed in faith for her child, but if somebody's anointed to minister that way, it's a whole lot better."

Yes, he could have prayed the prayer of faith — any one of us ministers standing there that night could have prayed the prayer of faith and laid hands on the child. The laying on of hands belongs to all believers according to Mark 16:17,18.

But what was Brother Carter recognizing? He was recognizing that in the ministry some of us are anointed to do one thing and some are anointed to do another, and if we'll excel where our anointing is, we'll be a greater blessing to the Body of Christ.

No one is going to do it all. We need each other. I praise God for every ministry called of God and anointed with the Holy Spirit.

The Offices of Evangelist and Exhorter

Actually, the healing ministry — *the gifts of healings* (1 Cor. 12:28) — should go with the office of the *evangelist*.

The Word of God also talks about the office of the *exhorter* (Rom. 12:8). We usually think of exhortation as being part of all these other offices, but there is a specific office of exhorter.

Those whom we call "evangelists" often are exhorters

(I know it would hurt their feelings to tell them that).

The word "evangelist," however, is used only three times in the New Testament: (1) "Philip the evangelist" is spoken of in Acts 21:8; (2) the gift "evangelist" is listed in Ephesians 4:11; (3) and Paul told Timothy to do "the work of an evangelist" in Second Timothy 4:5.

Philip, then, is the only model other than Jesus that we have for an evangelist.

In the early days of the Church, we see that Philip went down to Samaria and preached with great miracles resulting. At that time, however, as we will study in Chapter 8, Philip was still a deacon.

> ACTS 8:5-7
> 5 Then Philip went down to the city of Samaria, and preached Christ unto them.
> 6 And the people with one accord gave heed unto those things which Philip spake, hearing and seeing the miracles which he did [which HE DID!].
> 7 For unclean spirits, crying with loud voice, came out of many that were possessed with them: and many taken with palsies, and that were lame, were healed.

There's no doubt Philip was anointed by the Holy Spirit. Many who had the palsy were healed, the Bible says. Many who were lame were healed. It doesn't mention anything about anybody else being healed, but those healings were enough to attract attention to Jesus. People got saved, *"and there was great joy in that city"* (v. 8).

Notice that not *all* of the people were healed. Verse 7 says *"MANY . . . were healed."* If *everybody* had gotten healed of *all* kinds of diseases, the Bible would have said so.

The Bible says of the ministry of Jesus, *"And Jesus went about all Galilee, . . . healing ALL manner of sickness and ALL manner of disease among the people"* (Matt. 4:23).

It's very interesting to notice how Jesus ministered. I wish we had time to trace it. Jesus ministered under the anointing in all five pivotal offices. Because Jesus had the Spirit *without measure,* all manner of sickness and all manner of disease were healed under His ministry, as we have seen.

Remember, Acts 10:38 said, *"How God ANOINTED* [there it is again] *Jesus of Nazareth with the Holy Ghost and with power: who went about doing good, and healing all that were oppressed of the devil."*

But any teacher of the Word could teach God's Word, or any preacher of the Word could preach God's Word, and people could believe that Word and be saved and healed *without any transfer of anointing.* (Of course, it's the Holy Spirit who anoints the teacher and preacher.)

Ministering under the anointing, however, is a different thing. God uses people differently. Notice that under Philip's ministry, *"unclean spirits... came out of many... and many taken with palsies, and that were lame, were healed."*

Why? *Because Philip was gifted to minister only in those areas of healing.*

Our RHEMA Bible Training Center students all have read F. F. Bosworth's classic book, *Christ the Healer.* I knew Bosworth. I've talked to him personally. He was 77 years old the last time I talked to him, but you'd have thought he was 55 just to look at him.

I heard him minister in another man's meeting. Bosworth would teach in the daytime and this other man would minister in the night services.

Bosworth would say, "Anybody who's deaf or has any ear trouble, even if you've had an operation and had your eardrum removed, come up here and I'll lay hands on you and you'll be healed." Every single one of the people Bosworth prayed for — without fail — got healed.

Bosworth said, "I can't tell you why — I don't know why — but God uses me along that line. I usually never fail to get a deaf person healed, or one whose hearing is impaired healed, or God will put a new eardrum in there if they've had an operation." Bosworth was endowed by the Spirit to minister in that area.

When Bosworth said he didn't understand it, that started me thinking. If there's something I don't know, I'll stay up day and night and burn the midnight oil until I find the answers. That's just my nature.

We ministers used to compare notes at Voice of Healing conventions that were held during the great Healing Revival. One preacher had great success in getting "deaf and dumb" (mute) people healed. Another said, "I don't remember of one deaf or dumb person being healed in my ministry, but nearly every blind person I lay hands on gets healed." The first man, who got deaf and dumb persons healed, couldn't remember of a blind person ever being healed under his ministry.

In comparing notes, I discovered that I got more people healed of cancer (usually in tumor form) than all the rest of them put together. I'd seldom fail along that line with a tumor or growth in those days; that's where my gift lay.

Minister where your anointing is — find out where it is.

Chapter 6
The Anointing To Preach

I remember how it shocked my Grandma when I announced, "I'm going to be a preacher."

Grandma said, "Why, son, you can't preach — you can't talk!"

It was true. Because my heart didn't beat right and I would pass out if I tried to exert myself, I had learned in my younger years to sit around and keep my mouth shut.

In fact, the year before I became bedfast, Grandpa Drake said one night at the supper table, "I saw your teacher Miss Bessie Mae Hamilton today, and I asked, 'How is Kenneth doing?'

" 'Oh,' she said, 'Mr. Drake, he's just like he always was. If you waited on him to say anything, he'd never say anything. In fact, he could miss the class and nobody would ever know it.' "

That put an idea in my mind! I decided to try that out. I had only two classes in the afternoon — Miss Bessie Mae's and another — so two or three times a week I'd play hooky and go to the show.

You know, they never did miss me. They never counted me absent. Of course, after I got saved, I quit doing that. When I went back to high school after my healing, I never missed a day. But that's how quiet I was.

After I was saved and healed, I began to preach as a young Baptist boy preacher. I knew I was called to preach, and the anointing to preach would come upon me. I didn't have any anointing to teach, and I didn't like teaching.

I'd pray, study, and prepare sermon outlines — and I've got nearly all of them still. I don't preach some of them anymore, but they represent all the light I had then. (God will bless you because you're walking in all the light you have.)

The first time I preached, I preached 45 minutes. Some beginners go 10 or 15 minutes. I went 45. And I've been going ever since!

For a number of years I was a preacher — and, oh, I could preach! I was a preaching machine! I liked that anointing! When it came upon me, I'd preach so hard and fast, the congregation would say, "Slow down! Slow down! We can't get half of what you say, you go so fast."

I didn't have the baptism in the Holy Spirit then, but I had the Holy Spirit *in* me, and an anointing would come *on* me, because I was called to that office. (In the Old Testament, too, the anointing came *on* people to stand in certain offices.)

The Glory Cloud Manifests

I could relate some phenomenal things that happened when the anointing to preach came upon me as a young Baptist boy preacher.

One Sunday night I was preaching an evangelistic-type sermon from James 4:14, where James asks, *"For what is your life? It is even a vapour, that appeareth for a little time, and then vanisheth away."* I'd been preaching about 15 minutes, anointed by the Holy Spirit, when the power of God came into that church auditorium and filled it like a cloud.

I could not see a single member — I was in the cloud. I could hear the sound of my voice, but I didn't know one word of what I said. For 17 minutes — I looked at my watch — I couldn't distinguish a word.

Finally I could see people on the first three rows of seats. Then the anointing began to go away. It was just like a cloud lifted from the whole group. I didn't say anything about it; I closed the service normally.

Several days later I asked a very spiritual old gentleman who had been there, "Was anything different about the service Sunday night?"

"Well, why?" he replied.

"Well, you tell me if there was, and then I'll tell you why."

He said, "Well, the only thing was that people have been talking about it all over the community. It seemed like your face shone. It didn't look like you — it just looked like the face of an angel."

Then I told him about it. I told him I hadn't known one word I said for the last 17 minutes of the service, the anointing was upon me so. That's all a work of the Holy Spirit: the anointing and the glory cloud.

The Anointing Increases

After being baptized in the Holy Spirit, I entered into a greater dimension of the power of God, and that anointing to preach increased.

There is a scriptural basis for this: Elisha desired a double portion of Elijah's anointing. Elijah was anointed by the Holy Spirit to stand in the office of prophet, and Elisha had a double portion of that anointing — a greater anointing, in other words, to stand in the same office.

After I was baptized with the Holy Spirit and spoke in tongues, I didn't announce it to my church. I followed that anointing in me that teaches you all things.

Something on the inside of me said, "Don't say anything about it in church." So I never mentioned it; I just went right on with our services in that little country church.

It wasn't 30 days until people started saying, "What happened to you?"

"What do you mean, what happened to me?"

"Well, you're different," they said.

"What do you mean, I'm different? Is it good or bad?"

"It's good," they said.

"Well," I said, "what is it? What do you mean?"

"Oh, you've got power you didn't have before. When you preach, you have power you didn't have before."

I had been anointed to preach before, but now the anointing to preach was increased.

The people said, "When you preach now, it almost knocks us off the seats."

They didn't mean I was a hard preacher — it was just the power behind the preaching.

One member of the congregation was a Presbyterian. Ours was a community church — the only church in the community — and 85 percent of the people were Baptists.

This Presbyterian gentleman was wealthy even for that day. He owned many acres of land. All of his children were grown and married. Just before he and his wife left on a tour to Europe, he had heard of a couple in the community who had received the baptism in the Holy Spirit, and he had announced, "If that talking in tongues gets in here, I'm pulling all of my folks out!" There were seven families of them.

While he was in Europe, I received the baptism. When

he returned, he asked another member, an elderly Methodist man, "What happened to our little preacher while I was gone?"

This Methodist gentleman was a spiritual giant. He told me he had answered, "Oh, has something happened to him?"

"Yes, it sure has," the Presbyterian said.

"What do you mean?"

"Well, he's a better preacher than he used to be."

"Well, I always thought he was a good preacher," the Methodist answered.

"Yeah, but he's more powerful now than he ever was before. He's got a power he never had before."

I had shared my experience with the Methodist man, although I hadn't told it publicly, because I didn't want the church split.

So he said, "Mr. C., you know what happened to our little preacher while you were gone?"

"No."

"He got baptized with the Holy Spirit and spoke in other tongues!"

The Presbyterian dropped his head, and the Methodist didn't know if he was about to announce he was pulling out or not.

But we never lost a member, we never lost a family. They saw the value of the experience.

The Presbyterian announced, "I've heard him preach before, and I've heard him preach since, and I want it!"

Ninety-three percent of them followed me in the baptism of the Holy Spirit, and the other seven percent still attended.

Although I would be anointed to preach, that strong

anointing with the glory cloud didn't happen again in my ministry for three more years. During those years I had been baptized in the Holy Spirit, had come over among Full Gospel people, and was pastoring a little church in the black land of northcentral Texas.

One Sunday night I was preaching away on prophecy — it was the second Sunday night of September 1939 — and the anointing came upon me. I don't know what I said, and I couldn't see anything or anyone. It was as if a cloud or dense fog filled the church.

When I came to myself, I was standing down in front, off the platform. That was the first time I'd ever done that. In fact, my wife had said, "I believe you could preach standing in a wash pan," because I never moved from behind the pulpit when I preached. I had been trained that way when I was a Southern Baptist.

But here the glory had come down and I didn't know one word I had said for 15 minutes. I had been in the glory cloud. When I found myself walking around the altar, I got so embarrassed my face got red, and I ran back on the platform, got behind the pulpit, said, "Amen. Let's pray," and gave the invitation.

When the Anointing Is Present

Every sinner in the church came and got saved. We had revival that night! Twenty were baptized in the Holy Spirit that night. That may not sound big now, but back in 1939 if we had half a dozen saved and three baptized in the Holy Spirit, we thought we had a landslide.

In that service everybody who didn't have the baptism was baptized, and everybody who was lost or backslid got

back to God. It wasn't my preaching that did it; it was
the anointing.

The glory cloud still appears quite frequently in our
healing meetings and other services. People have seen it.
It comes in and fills the room.

Sometimes when I am preaching or teaching, it comes
in and absolutely blocks everyone from view. Most of the
time it just hangs above their heads. It is at times like
these that people receive healing without anyone ministering to them, because the anointing is there.

Sometimes the anointing comes into visible manifestation. Do you think it wasn't *visible* when the house started
shaking where the early Christians were praying? And
when that jail at Philippi started shaking and every door
flew open, it came into manifestation again as a result of
Paul's and Silas' praying.

I have the anointing of the Holy Spirit in me all the
time, as any believer has, but we're speaking here of an
anointing to preach.

I don't preach much anymore — I mostly teach — but
I like the preaching anointing. I *love* it.

It's different from the anointing to teach. It feels different. It's more exuberant. *It's the same Spirit, but a
different anointing.* Thank God for the anointing to preach!
If I had any control over it, I'd bring on that anointing
to preach often, because I like it.

The difference between preaching and teaching is that
to preach means to *proclaim,* but to teach means to
explain.

Once in a while, that anointing to preach still will come
on me. If you've never heard me preach, get my tape "El
Shaddai." I'm preaching on that one, not teaching.

I preached "El Shaddai" years ago at a Full Gospel Business Men's meeting near Washington, D.C. The special singer was singing the last song, and I was sitting there on that platform minding my own business, ready to give my testimony about going to hell, when something like a cloak came on me. It fit over me like an overcoat. It was this anointing to preach. You talk about a fellow feeling "preachy"!

Remember, Elijah threw his cloak over Elisha, signifying that the Holy Spirit was coming on him in that way: just like a mantle was on him, and that's the way it was with me. After all, these Old Testament types and shadows were fulfilled in the New.

When they turned the service over to me, I didn't have my sermon notes on "El Shaddai," but the anointing was there to preach, so I just took my text and took off. We had a service!

Chapter 7
The Anointing To Teach

Even though I wasn't a teacher to begin with, I always had the greatest respect for the Word of God, and always was very studious. I spent hours studying and reading, digging things out for myself in my early years as a pastor, but I didn't teach those things. I had no unction or leading to teach.

I did teach a Bible class in the church, however. That's the custom in most Pentecostal churches. Sometimes Full Gospel, Pentecostal people criticize denominational people for formality and ritualism, yet Pentecostals are bound with customs! They'll fight for their customs. All these things are bad.

I received the baptism of the Holy Spirit and spoke in other tongues in 1937, and in 1939, as I say humorously, I received "the left foot of fellowship" from among the Baptists and came over among the Pentecostals. My wife and I accepted the pastorate of a little Pentecostal church in North Texas.

The people said, "It's a custom that the pastor teach the men's Bible class and the pastor's wife teach the older ladies' Bible class."

"Well," I replied, "I just changed the custom." I hadn't been around Pentecostals too long at that stage, and I thought they were all sprouting wings. I found out later those were just their shoulder blades sticking out. They weren't about to grow any wings. And I found out if you start changing their customs, you're in for it.

So I had to maneuver and speak softly, but finally I got it over to them that my wife didn't teach. They said, "Well, we'll tell you what we'll do. We'll just combine the older men and the older ladies and have an auditorium class, and you teach it." I'd rather have done almost anything else, but I taught it.

I never was so glad of anything in my life as I was when that class was over each Sunday morning. I'd lay that teacher's quarterly down and say, "Whew, now I can relax for another week."

I so detested teaching that I wouldn't look at the Sunday School quarterly for the whole week. Sometimes I didn't pick it up to study it until just before the class started the next Sunday morning!

I could get by with that because I had developed a unique ability — after I was born again — of being able to read something once and never forget it. I didn't have that talent before I got born again. But afterwards I could read a chapter in my high school history book once and recite it word for word for the teacher. It was because I learned to walk in the life of God. Doing that will increase your mentality. I could hardly remember anything before.

So I could read the teacher's lesson once from the quarterly and rattle it off. Then I'd say, "I'm glad that's over! Now I can get back to preaching!" And I'd preach up a storm, going like an air hammer, waving my arms like a windmill. (I thought it wasn't preaching unless you did that.) I was a preacher, and I loved it. I'd have rather preached than eaten.

I preached for nine years. All I had was the evangelistic message. I never preached anything else. I didn't *have* anything else!

But I remember one Thursday afternoon at 3 o'clock. (The year was 1943. I had been preaching since 1934.)

I'd been lying down. I walked across the parsonage

living room and into the kitchen for a drink of water. As I was coming back across the living room, right in the middle of the room, something dropped down on me and inside me. It just clicked down on the inside of me like a coin drops inside a pay phone. I stopped dead still. I knew what it was. It was a teaching gift. The anointing to teach had dropped inside me. I said, "Now I can teach."

If I get any gift from God, I prove it out first, and I would encourage you to do the same. Prove what you've got from God, and then you can talk about it. But if it's never proved, proclaiming it won't make it so. I never said a word about having the anointing to teach.

We had a little prayer group of seven or eight women who met Wednesday afternoons from 2 to 4 at the church. People would turn in requests and they would pray over the requests and pray about the church and the services for a few hours. My wife always met with them, and I usually met with them.

We trained this little group to pray. They became expert prayer warriors. If you didn't want something, you'd better not turn in a prayer request to them, because they'd get it for you!

I suggested to them that we have a Bible lesson for an hour before our prayer time, but I didn't invite anybody else to come. It wasn't an announced meeting.

I started teaching those seven or eight women, and the anointing would come on me. I hadn't known you could stand in one spot and just teach the Word and get that strongly anointed to teach. I thought you were supposed to be hollering at the top of your voice, waving your arms like a windmill, and "spitting cotton," as in preaching.

But just standing there with a handful, teaching them

the Word, the anointing would come on me so strongly I couldn't stand it. I'd have to say, "Lord, turn it off — I can't stand it anymore!"

You talk about getting blessed! It was like getting hold of electric current. That anointing and the Word flowed out to the women. They went home and told their husbands and others. Still we never announced the Wednesday afternoon Bible study. Nobody was invited to come.

But people started coming Wednesday afternoons in spite of the fact that we had regular Wednesday night services, too. The women's husbands would take off from work to get in on that afternoon service. It wasn't long until we filled the building. We had a bigger crowd Wednesday afternoon than we did Wednesday night!

I proved my teaching gift. It worked. I started out by faith and kept going, and the building filled up in the afternoon. That proved the gift, didn't it?

I began to do more and more teaching as a pastor until the ratio was probably about half teaching and half preaching. Now I seldom get the anointing to preach anymore. Thank God for that teaching anointing! It's a little different, but it's still the same Spirit who anoints you for whatever He calls you to do.

Chapter 8
The Anointing To Pastor

The word "pastor" appears only once in *The King James Version*. That's amazing, when it's such an important office and so widespread — more so than any other office.

The sole reference is in Ephesians 4:11: *"And he gave some, . . . pastors . . . ."* However, we can find references to this office elsewhere in Scripture because the Greek word translated "pastor" also is translated "shepherd."

Something else you need to understand to save you from confusion is the fact that the Greek word *episkopos* translated "bishop" is also translated "overseer," for they are the same word. Both words also mean "pastor."

In his farewell message to the elders, Paul said to the Church at Ephesus, *"Take heed therefore unto yourselves, and to all the flock, over the which the Holy Ghost hath made you OVERSEERS, to feed the church of God, which he hath purchased with his own blood"* (Acts 20:28). These elders were pastors.

Great controversy has come concerning elders. Study Early Church history and you'll discover that the Greek word translated "elder" simply means "an older person."

In the beginning days of the Church, they didn't have all of the ministries listed in the New Testament. The only ministries the Church had in the beginning were the apostles.

Then came the great persecution in Jerusalem, and the early Christians were scattered abroad. They went everywhere preaching Jesus, and every one of them was a preacher.

Acts 8:5 says that *"Philip went down to Samaria and*

preached Christ unto them." But Philip was not an evangelist then. The apostles had laid hands on him and he was set into the office of deacon first.

Later, in the 21st chapter of Acts, we read that Luke and Paul and their company went down to Caesarea and were in the house of *"Philip the evangelist."* When God began to raise up ministries, He made an evangelist out of Philip.

It takes time to develop ministries. You may get saved — and even baptized in the Holy Spirit — today, and the call of God may be on you to be a pastor, but you can't start pastoring tomorrow, dear friends. You're not ready for it. You'll have to be prepared for it.

So start out to obey God, whether you're in the ministry or not, and God will promote you and use you in a greater way. If you, like Philip, learn to be faithful wherever you are, God may see fit to move you on. If He does, fine. If He doesn't, just stay faithful where you are. He'll not be able to use you if you're not faithful.

In the Early Church, because there was a lack of ministries, they would appoint an elder ("an older person") over a particular flock. Out of these elders God developed pastors or overseers.

It is certainly unscriptural to take a layman who has no anointing upon him and put him in the office of an elder or make him overseer of a congregation. He doesn't have the anointing to do it. He only has an anointing like any other believer.

So we see that the *bishop, overseer,* or *elder* is the same office: the *pastoral* office.

Who has the oversight of the flock? The shepherd does. What does "shepherd" mean? The Greek word translated "shepherd" is translated "pastor." Who, then, would oversee the flock? The shepherd would. Jesus is called by Peter *"the Shepherd and Bishop of your souls"* (1 Peter 2:25).

And in First Peter 5:4 we read, *"And when the CHIEF SHEPHERD shall appear, ye shall receive a crown of glory that fadeth not away."*

Jesus is the Great Shepherd, the Chief Shepherd, of all God's sheep. Jesus has under shepherds. A pastor is an under shepherd. A pastor is a shepherd of God's sheep.

God calls and equips men to shepherd, or pastor, a flock.

*   *   *   *   *

Prophecy

Many would say, "Let's get back to the Acts of the Apostles. Let's get back to the Early Church. Let's do things like they did."

Yes, saith the Spirit of God, have the same experience they did — walk in the same light they did — but if you walk in the same church government they walked in, you'll be a baby church and a baby Christian with no spiritual growth.

But you have grown and you have developed. Therefore, rise up and walk in the light of the Word of God for today.

Enjoy the full flow of the Spirit of God, and the anointing of God will rest upon thee; and the anointing of God will flow through thee; and the anointing of God will be UPON MEN as they stand in the place of ministry.

And so shall the entire Church be edified and the work of God shall be wrought.

*   *   *   *   *

What I Learned as a Pastor

I don't know a lot about the anointing of the pastor, even though I pastored about 12 years.

You might say, "Well, you pastored — you ought to know."

I would have to reply, "That wasn't my office."

I did function in that office temporarily as God permitted me to, but I didn't have the anointing to pastor. It's a different anointing. *It's the same Spirit, but it's a different anointing.*

I recognize it on people, and I'm blessed by it, but I don't have it and never did have it. Thank God for the pastor. Thank God for the pastoral office. It's a marvelous anointing and blessing of God. It's amazing how the anointing — the Spirit of God — comes upon a person to stand in the office of pastor.

Some claim to be pastors. If you're called of God to pastor, the anointing is going to be there to pastor.

There's more to pastoring than preaching, however. The anointing is not there all the time to preach. If it were, a fellow would preach himself to death. But the anointing will come on you when you come to the pulpit to preach.

Paul wrote to Timothy, a young pastor, *"Study to shew thyself approved unto God, a workman that needeth not to be ashamed, rightly dividing the word of truth"* (2 Tim. 2:15).

I learned a lot during the time God permitted me to pastor. I think every pastor ought to be forced out on the field to evangelize or be in field ministry for at least two years. Then he'd know how to entertain evangelists and special speakers.

On the other hand, I think evangelists ought to be forced into pastoring at least two years. Then they wouldn't say a lot of things they say sometimes.

After about 10 years of pastoral work, I shut myself up in my church and prayed and fasted for days. I said, "Lord, why am I so dissatisfied? The church is growing. We've got all the money we need. We have the best parsonage we've ever lived in. We've got the best of everything.

"People are getting saved, filled with the Holy Spirit, and healed in our services. From the natural standpoint, we have every reason in the world to be satisfied — but I'm not satisfied. Something is not right."

I kept seeking God. One day as I was praying around the altar, God said, "The reason is, I never did call you to pastor to begin with. That's not your calling. That's not your office."

Did you know there are a lot of people in the wrong office? And it's dangerous — really dangerous — to intrude into another office.

Ministering in the Wrong Office

In Old Testament days, if you intruded into another office, you fell dead instantly. Two fellows intruded into the Holy Place and fell dead instantly, for example.

In these days of grace — thank God for grace — you can get by with it longer, but you can't get by with it forever. Sooner or later, as the Bible says, if you don't judge yourself, you'll have to be judged so you won't be condemned with the world:

1 CORINTHIANS 11:31,32

31 For if we would judge ourselves, we should not be judged.

32 But when we are judged, we are chastened of the Lord, that we should not be condemned with the world.

Through my 50 years in the ministry, I've known mighty men of God — and I mean *mighty* men — who were anointed by the Holy Spirit to function in such offices as prophet and evangelist, with the working of miracles, gifts of healings, and the gift of special faith manifested through them. Some of them ought to be alive still today, but they're dead because they tried to function — *and had no anointing to function* — over in another office.

If they had stayed in their own office, they wouldn't have died prematurely. You can add to or diminish the anointing. The anointing they had diminished.

One day Gordon Lindsay, founder of Christ for the Nations, and I were discussing one of the outstanding ministers who had died — one who had stood at the forefront of the Healing Revival. We were all in the Voice of Healing organization at one time.

God had told me two years before that this minister was going to die — and he died exactly when the Lord said he would.

Somebody asked me, "Why didn't you go tell him?"

The Lord didn't tell me to tell him. In fact, the witness of my spirit was, "Leave him alone. Don't say a word to him." But because Brother Lindsay was closer to the man, the Holy Spirit told him four times to go tell him, "You're going to die." Brother Lindsay, too, saw that he wouldn't listen, so he just kept quiet about it.

He had dealt with the minister earlier on this subject,

pleading with him, "Why don't you function where God wants you and manifest the gift that God's given you. Stay there. Don't try to get over here in this other ministry."

The man would try to teach. He wasn't a teacher. That wasn't his calling. He had no unction, no anointing, to teach, and he would create confusion instead of blessing.

He answered Brother Lindsay, "Yeah, but I want to teach."

Don't be a teacher just because you *want* to be one! Have the call and the anointing of God to do it, or else leave it alone. And if the anointing's there to preach, don't try to teach. Don't try to stand in an office unless the anointing and the call are there.

"Yeah, but . . . " the man said, "I want to." And the man died. He ought to still be alive. He could have been a great blessing.

I've seen marvelous ministries like his ruined and the Church robbed of the blessings she ought to have had because people didn't minister under their anointing. You can spread yourself so thin in different ministries that you get very little anointing on any of them.

That's one reason I stay over where the Lord called me, whether I'm preaching or teaching. It doesn't make any difference what I'm teaching on or where I start out — I wind up preaching on faith and healing. Just as soon as I get on those subjects, I'm gone. I could start preaching on the anti-Christ and wind up preaching on faith and healing.

God may lead you to speak on different subjects at certain times, especially if you're a pastor. He never called me to pastor, although I did function there for a while, and thank God for it. It was a learning period, but it still wasn't my calling.

Back in 1948, somebody came along mightily used of God and anointed to minister healing. A pastor friend told me, "Brother Hagin, you could do that. The same anointing that's on him is on you."

I hadn't thought a thing about such a ministry; I was still pastoring.

My friend said, "When you preach for me and get on the subject of healing or faith, it's just like a dog on a rabbit's trail. You just take off!"

That was because God was going to anoint me to do what He had called me to do. If I had persisted in doing something else, like pastoring, the anointing wouldn't be there and I would have diminished the overall anointing upon my life and ministry.

I preached my farewell sermon at my last pastorate the first Sunday of February 1949.

When the Lord appeared to me in that first vision in 1950 in the Rockwall, Texas, tent meeting, He said, among other things, "When you left your last church, at that time you entered into the first phase of your ministry."

At that time I had already been in the ministry 15 years (from 1934 to 1949). Twelve years of it had been in pastoral work. The rest had been in evangelistic work. And I'm not an evangelist either — that's not my calling. (That's the reason the anointing to preach won't come on me very often.)

So when the Lord said I had entered into the first phase of my ministry when I left my last church, I argued with Him about it. (Ananias argued with Him, too, over going to pray for Saul of Tarsus.)

I said, "Lord, that can't be so. You mean I preached 15 years in the ministry and never even got into the *first* phase of the ministry You have for me?"

He said, "That's exactly right."

Then He said something we all need to think about. He said, "*Many ministers live and die and never even get into the first phase of the ministry I have for them. Not always, but many times that's the reason they die young or in middle life and don't live their full length of time out.*"

If you're not in God's best, you can't claim God's best. If you're not in God's perfect will, you can't claim His perfect provision. We need to know that and find our place.

Often God will let you serve nearly anywhere during a period of training. But *the time will come that you need to get on your knees and find your place.*

Here's where we miss it: Instead of doing this, we think, *Well, I'm in the ministry — I'm working for God —* and we find our own place. But you can die working for God!

You must ask yourself, "What did He *call* me to do? What does He *want* me to do?"

Oh, I never want to do something just because *I* want to do it. I want to obey God.

Well, the anointing came on me to teach, so I began to teach. I didn't have any anointing then to stand in the office of the prophet, although I prophesied.

Chapter 9
The Anointing of the Prophet

Jesus had *all* of the anointings combined to stand in *all* of the offices.

Paul, writing to Timothy, said concerning his own ministry, *"I am appointed a PREACHER, and an APOSTLE, and a TEACHER to the Gentiles"* (2 Tim. 1:11). We know from Acts 13 that Paul also stood in the office of prophet.

We know that Paul stood in the office of prophet because he had visions and revelations. A prophet is one who has visions and revelations, among other things. All of the Gospel Paul learned he learned that way.

Some of us, like Paul, stand in more than one office. Often we'll weave in and out of these offices.

Thank God I had the anointing to preach and then the anointing to teach. I continued to preach and teach. I spoke in tongues and prophesied, but I never stood in the office of prophet until 1952. I know exactly when I entered into the ministry of the prophet.

I don't have the anointing of the apostle or the pastor — I never have had them — but I recognize those anointings on others.

The anointing of the prophet is the same Holy Spirit, but a different anointing.

It is important to notice that there is a difference between: (1) *standing in the office of a prophet,* and (2) *the simple gift of prophecy.*

Every Spirit-filled believer could prophesy and could know something about the anointing to prophesy. The Bible teaches that: *"For ye may all prophesy one by one, that all may learn, and all may be comforted"* (1 Cor. 14:31).

The simple gift of prophecy is speaking to men to *edification, exhortation,* and *comfort.* A good testimony, inspired by the Holy Spirit, is the simple gift of prophecy. So you see, just prophesying doesn't make you a prophet! It's the Spirit within you who anoints you to prophesy, yet there is also an anointing or ministry gift to stand in the office of a prophet.

Thank God for the anointing of the prophet. Oh, I love it! Often, sitting on the platform before I take the service to teach, I suddenly sense that prophetic anointing — *the office of the prophet* — moving upon me. I recognize what it is.

It's a different anointing. It's deeper — much deeper — than the anointing just to prophesy. It's the same anointing, because it's the same Spirit, but *it's multiplied about a hundredfold.*

I have found that the anointing can be stronger or it can be weaker, as we will see in the story of Elisha and Elijah, the two Old Testament prophets.

If I were controlling things, I'd prophesy in every service, but that may not be what God wants in every service.

The first time I experienced this overwhelming anointing to prophesy was in January 1964 in Phoenix, Arizona. I was there to be one of the speakers at the Full Gospel Business Men's Convention.

After the closing session, Brother and Sister Darrell Hon, their son Barry, and my wife and I went to a nearby restaurant to get something to eat. Before we ordered, the Spirit of God suddenly came on me. I recognized it as the spirit of prophecy — a better term is "the spirit of the prophet."

I said to our party, "Let's go somewhere where we can

pray." We went to our motel room, sat down, and prayed a while. The anointing had broken a little by our getting up and leaving the restaurant, but by praying it returned.

For two hours I sat there and prophesied. I'd never prophesied that long in my life. Brother Hon wrote it down, for we didn't have a tape recorder with us. He got most of it.

I've never had an experience exactly like this. I've had two similar experiences since then, but not with the same measure of anointing.

It seemed as if I were sitting beside myself on the edge of that bed. It seemed as if there were two of me. I was listening with my physical ears to what this fellow sitting beside me said.

It seemed to me that I had nothing whatsoever to do with what he was saying. It seemed as if I were completely taken over by the Spirit of God. Once I began to yield to the Spirit, it was the easiest thing in the world.

For two hours the Lord took us through the years 1964, 1965, 1966, 1967, and 1968: five years. He told us what was going to happen in Vietnam, and He told us what was going to happen with our government.

He also told us that a man who stood in the forefront of the ministry would be taken. I still have the prophecy as Brother Hon took it down.

It reads, "Satan shall destroy his life. His soul shall be saved and his work shall follow him. Ere 1966 shall come, he shall be gone." It happened. It wasn't God's full plan or full purpose for him, but nonetheless it happened.

I experienced a similar overwhelming anointing on April 30, 1980, while teaching at our Prayer and Healing School on the RHEMA campus in Tulsa, Oklahoma. (It happens to me sometimes in preaching, but more often in teaching.)

Let me show you something about the prophet's ministry. I don't operate there all the time, but neither did Elijah and Elisha.

Suddenly while *teaching* the Word (I'm a teacher so I can operate in that office all the time), I moved over into this other area. Right in front of me, with my eyes wide open, I had what I call a "mini-vision."

As if it had literally happened, I saw a young woman standing in the aisle. I saw myself point to her and say, "Be healed in the Name of Jesus!" I saw her go over backwards.

I saw men standing in both aisles, so I stopped and acted that out, too. (I frequently act out these mini-visions.) I said to them, "Stand in the aisle. Be healed in the Name of Jesus!"

That's the only time I've ever done that. I don't know if I'll ever do it again or not, but I will if the Lord says to. In fact, He didn't say to then; I just saw it in the mini-vision. Both men went over backwards. I simply acted out that mini-vision — or so I thought.

When you have faith to move into the realm of the Spirit and obey Him, He'll take you on. If He showed you everything before you moved, you would not be walking by faith, you'd be walking by sight, and that would not please Him. So you'll never know everything.

But if you'll have the faith to step out when the Spirit moves, He'll move you and you'll minister in the depth of the Spirit that you've never ministered in before; and the anointing of God shall not only come upon you and rest, but the anointing of God will be made manifest through you.

I remembered that first part of the mini-vision and would tell it. I don't mean I was unconscious of what happened next, but you can get off in the realm of the Spirit until you're so conscious of spiritual things that you don't even realize natural things.

(Now, you can fall into a trance, but I didn't fall into a trance on that occasion. I've fallen into a trance several times and have had visions. When you fall into a trance, your physical senses are suspended. You don't know where you are at the moment.)

Our staff asked me, "Brother Hagin, why don't you ever tell all of that story?"

I said, "Is there more to tell?"

"Yes," they said. "You leave that woman lying back there in the aisle."

"Well, wasn't that the end of it?"

"No," they said. "That's part of it, but it didn't end there."

I asked them to tell me what happened, for I had no knowledge of the rest of the story.

They said, "After you acted that part out, you called the woman up to the front, and we never saw you act that way before.

"You jumped off the platform and grabbed the woman like a cat grabbing a mouse. You laid one hand on her stomach and one hand on her back, shook her, cast three devils out of her — fear, death, and disease — and commanded her to be healed. She fell to the floor the second time and lay there until 6 p.m."

When she went back to the doctor, he couldn't find a trace of cancer. It had all disappeared. The woman was completely healed of cancer. Her testimony appeared in the December 1981 issue of our magazine, *The Word of Faith*. The woman and her husband later moved to Tulsa and attended RHEMA Bible Training Center in preparation for the ministry.

After my staff told me what happened, I had only the faintest recollection of it — it was like a dream to me. It seemed as if I had been taken over by the Spirit of God. (You have to be willing to be used and you have to yield to Him.)

I've also been *preaching* when the anointing to stand in the office of prophet suddenly came on me (it already was on me to preach). I don't control this anointing — God does.

Once while preaching I suddenly was standing on a street corner miles away. I could hear the sound of my voice continuing to preach, but I don't know to this day a single word of what I said, because I was standing on that street corner.

I saw a mini-vision of a woman from my congregation walking down the street. I saw a man pull up to the curb in his automobile and sound the horn. The woman got in the car and they drove out in the country. I was sitting in the back seat. They committed adultery.

Suddenly I was conscious of being behind the pulpit again. I saw that woman sitting before me in the congregation. Now, God didn't show that incident to me to reveal it in front of everybody. In fact, I never said a word to anybody. He showed it to me in order to restore her — to get her back in fellowship with God.

Again, while preaching down in Alabama, the anointing suddenly came on me and I saw a mini-vision of two women having a fight. Down the street and about a block away I saw a church. Across the top I saw the name of it.

The two women tore each other's clothes off. One finally got loose and ran away. The other went down to a little white frame house that stood beside the church.

I was standing out in the yard with her, and I could see the outline of a man standing in the doorway. He hooked the screen door when he saw her.

She cursed him because he wouldn't agree that she was right in beating up that other woman. She threatened to come through the screen and whip him, too. He was ready to shut the door when she finally left.

And then I was back in the service, and there she stood in front of me in the prayer line, wanting to be baptized with the Holy Spirit.

I said, "You're not going to get baptized with the Holy Spirit until you get things straightened up." I talked to her about what I had seen.

The Full Gospel pastor of that church didn't understand that kind of a move of the Spirit. You see, *many churches believe in the gifts of the Spirit on paper, but not in action.*

When I told him what I had seen in the Spirit, he admitted he was the man who was standing in the doorway. The fight I had seen had actually happened.

Now I'll share with you another way the Holy Spirit moves with me sometimes, but not often. I "see" myself go down the aisles and lay hands on some of the people.

As I act this out and walk by people, it's just like a magnet draws me to them. When it does, I stop and minister to them. Thank God for the anointing!

I read where Smith Wigglesworth said, "I'd rather

have the Holy Ghost on me 10 minutes than to own the world with a fence around it." He was speaking about the anointing to minister.

As the Spirit Wills

I want you to notice something about the anointing of the prophet. Sometimes people think that if you're in a certain office, such as the office of the prophet, you stand in it all the time.

These people miss it because they fail to read what the Bible says, and they try to perform when the anointing's not there. They get in the flesh, prophesy, and do an injustice to the work of God. Or they seem to think that because you stand in the office of the prophet, you go around handing out revelations all the time.

I know one man, bless his heart, who has the anointing of God upon him, because supernatural things happen through his ministry — there's no doubt about it — but because he thinks he's called to the office of the prophet, he thinks he has to function in it all the time!

I remember the first time I met him. Within 30 minutes he must have given me 12 "words" from the Lord, and not one of them was correct. They didn't amount to the proverbial hill of beans.

I stand sometimes in the office of prophet, and some people think I stand in it all the time. They'll even lie to try to get through to me.

We were speaking out of town once and were awakened at 4 o'clock in the morning. We were told we had an emergency long distance call. We thought one of our relatives had died or something.

Instead there was some woman on the other end of the

line (sometimes it's a man). This one said, "Brother Hagin, I hated to do that, but it's the only way I could get through to you." (That's flat out lying.)

"You know," she continued, "I was praying and I thought I'd see if I could get hold of you. I thought maybe you'd have a word for me."

I wanted to say, "I have!" but I didn't have enough nerve to give it to her.

People think you can just turn it off and on as you want, but it is as the Spirit wills. Yes, the anointing is there *potentially,* but it's not in manifestation *constantly!* As you prepare, study, and yield to the Spirit of God, the anointing will be there to function in that office, but you don't stand in your office all the time.

Stop and think about that. If your office is the office of a teacher, and you functioned in that office all the time, you'd be teaching 24 hours a day, and you'd never stop until you died!

You really couldn't bear to stand in the office of a prophet 24 hours a day, even though the call might be there and the potential anointing might be there. The human body cannot contain that degree of spiritual power over a long period of time, as we will see in Chapter 14.

Jesus called Himself a prophet in the fourth chapter of Luke's Gospel, and He used an illustration that His Jewish audience knew well from the Old Covenant: the story of the Prophet Elijah, who was sent to the widow's house in Sarepta during a famine.

There the working of miracles was manifested through Elijah: The oil cruse kept giving out oil, and the meal barrel kept giving out meal (1 Kings 17:16). But Elijah couldn't go into anybody else's house in Israel and do that unless the Lord told him to.

Next Jesus related that there were many lepers in Israel in the time of Elisha (Luke 4:27), but none of them was healed, even though Elisha had a reputation of having a healing ministry.

We know that because of what the little Israeli maid said when she found out that her master, Naaman, had leprosy: *"Would God my lord were with the prophet that is in Samaria! for he would recover him of his leprosy"* (2 Kings 5:3).

Not one leper in Israel was healed, only Naaman from Syria — yet Elisha was standing in the office of the prophet!

Remember, we don't control the anointing. We must learn to flow with the Spirit. We must learn to minister under the anointing. I love that anointing!

Elijah was anointed by the Holy Spirit to stand in the office of prophet, but Elisha had twice the measure of that anointing — a double portion — to stand in that office. Therefore, we can see that one could be more anointed than others in the same office.

Music Enhances the Anointing

We need to understand the role music plays in affecting the prophet's ministry. The third chapter of Second Kings gives us an example from the ministry of the Prophet Elisha.

In Old Testament times, only the prophet, priest, and king were anointed by the Spirit to stand in those three offices. Otherwise, people didn't have the anointing of the Spirit of God on them unless God especially called them.

Therefore, if they needed to inquire of the Lord concerning some matter, they had to inquire through the prophet. (The prophet's ministry is different during this present dispensation.)

An enemy had come against the nation of Israel, which was divided at the time. Jehoshaphat, king of Judah, was conferring with two other kings — Jehoram, king of Israel, and the king of Edom, both of whom had forsaken God and were backslid.

Jehoshaphat asked, *"Is there not here a prophet of the Lord, that we may enquire of the Lord by him?"* (v. 11). One of the servants of the king of Israel mentioned Elisha, so the three kings went to him.

> **2 KINGS 3:13,14**
> 13 And Elisha said unto the king of Israel, What have I to do with thee? get thee to the prophets of thy father, and to the prophets of thy mother [because they had forsaken God]. And the king of Israel said unto him, Nay: for the Lord hath called these three kings together, to deliver them into the hand of Moab.
> 14 And Elisha said, As the Lord of hosts liveth, before whom I stand, surely, were it not that I regard the presence of Jehoshaphat the king of Judah, I would not look toward thee, nor see thee.

The Prophet Elisha regarded the presence of Jehoshaphat because God regarded the presence of Jehoshaphat. God will do a lot of things for his own people. Jehoshaphat wanted Elisha to prophesy regarding the outcome of the impending battle.

Elisha called for a minstrel, and his anointing was enhanced.

> **2 KINGS 3:15,16**
> 15 But now bring me a minstrel. And it came to pass,

WHEN THE MINSTREL PLAYED, THAT THE HAND OF THE LORD CAME UPON HIM.
16 And he said, Thus saith the Lord ....

Elisha went on to give the message of victory God gave him. *"The hand of the Lord came upon him."* Did you notice that? The "hand of the Lord" is the Holy Spirit, or we could say "the hand of the Lord" is *the anointing.*

Notice that *Elisha couldn't start prophesying any time he wanted to,* so he said, "Bring me a minstrel." And *the hand of the Lord came upon him when the minstrel played.*

Music comes under the ministry of helps listed in First Corinthians 12:28. The ministry of music is one of the greatest helps there is. Thank God for the ministry of music.

The Bible has much to say about music in connection with worship. We know that music helps us worship God. If you play the right kind of music in your home when you're praying or studying the Bible, what a difference it makes. When David would sing and play his harp, the evil spirit that troubled King Saul would depart.

Music affects all of the ministries; it has something to do with the anointing in all of the offices. Music can help all ministers — not just the prophet — because all ministers should minister under the anointing of the Holy Spirit.

The right kind of music and singing even will help the teacher teach better. However, it seems to me that music has more to do with the prophet's office than the others, because the prophet must be so sensitive to the Spirit.

We saw that as the minstrel played, "the hand of the Lord," or the anointing, came upon the Prophet Elisha and he began to prophesy.

Sometimes the anointing to stand in the office of prophet is so strong I don't need anything — I can step right into it. At other times, like Elisha, I need a little help.

Sometimes I'll have the singers and musicians sing and play. If they sing the wrong song, however, they'll kill the anointing (and the service). The words, tune, and rhythm may be right, but the song still may be out of place.

When this happens, the Spirit of God lifts from me — it goes as if it were a bird that flew away. No, the Holy Spirit doesn't stop indwelling me as a believer, but that anointing to minister lifts.

Music will affect the anointing. We are missing it in the area of the minstrel. Many times *musicians don't realize their responsibility.* They stand in the office of helps. They need to pray and get the anointing on them just as much as the preacher does. They need to develop a sensitivity to the Holy Spirit and learn how to flow with the Spirit.

Singers shouldn't get up and sing just to be singing. They need to be anointed. Even the choir should be anointed. But people don't stop to pray before ministering in song. They come into the church from everyday life, laughing and talking. That's all right in itself, because we need fellowship — but, really, that's carnal; it isn't spiritual. Before singers minister, they need to take time to get alone with God or take time to pray together to get the anointing on them.

I have found that when musicians really flow with the Spirit, it will cause the anointing to come on me stronger to stand in the office of the prophet.

I know what the Scripture means when it said the minstrel played and the hand of the Lord moved. There have been times when I have gotten the right kind of music, and I have moved over into the prophet's office and have ministered for as long as three hours. Prophecy just flowed out of me. I can't minister that way every time — even though I do minister in a certain measure of anointing — for there are measures of anointing.

The Right Song

In 1958, I was the main speaker at a convention being held in Kansas by the Foursquare denomination. One night the spirit of the prophet moved upon me. I can't bring it on myself, but I can yield to it when it comes, and music helps.

They had an orchestra there made up of people who had come from different churches. I said to them, "The anointing of the prophet is coming on me! Play something." They began to play "Preach the Word," a song written by Aimee Semple McPherson.

The anointing came on me and I ministered under it from 9 o'clock until midnight — three hours. Oh, what a service! I got caught up in the glory. Half the time I couldn't see. It was as if there were a hazy cloud over the whole room. I don't know to this day what I did or said. I just remember when the anointing came and when it lifted.

If they had played the wrong song, they would have killed the whole thing.

You see, it's necessary that singers and musicians be in tune with the Spirit of God as much as the minister is.

If they're not, everybody would be better off if there were no musicians participating in the service! (That's the reason I don't want any kind of singing sometimes.)

Other things affect the anointing as well. Often the spirit of the prophet will begin to move on me and something kills it. I think it's because of the environment, or maybe because of certain people present.

After all, Elisha said, "If it weren't for Jehoshaphat, I wouldn't look your way, as far as you other two kings are concerned." And because they were present in their backslidden condition, Elisha needed a little help.

"Bring me a minstrel . . . ," he said.

The Hand of the Lord

Again and again in the Old Testament we see references to "the hand of the Lord." Actually it is the Spirit of God — the anointing. Other terms commonly used are "Spirit," "double portion of thy Spirit," and "mantle." They're all referring to the Holy Spirit or the anointing of God.

> **EZEKIEL 8:1**
> 1 And it came to pass in the sixth year, in the sixth month, in the fifth day of the month, as I sat in mine house, and the elders of Judah sat before me, that THE HAND OF THE LORD FELL there upon me.

The call of God already was upon Ezekiel — the hand of God was upon him to minister *potentially* — but his prophetic ministry wasn't in manifestation until *the hand of the Lord fell* upon him.

(The Bible also speaks about the Holy Spirit "falling," doesn't it? In Acts 10:44, Peter was preaching in Cornelius' household, and *"While Peter yet spake these words, THE HOLY GHOST FELL on all them which heard the word."*)

We see the expression "hand of the Lord" used again in the 37th and 40th chapters of Ezekiel:

> **EZEKIEL 37:1**
> 1   THE HAND OF THE LORD was upon me, and car- ried me out in the spirit of the Lord, and set me down in the midst of the valley which was full of bones . . . . [Ezekiel had a vision of what we call the valley of dry bones.]

> **EZEKIEL 40:1,2**
> 1   In the five and twentieth year of our captivity, in the beginning of the year, in the tenth day of the month, in the fourteenth year after that the city was smitten, in the selfsame day THE HAND OF THE LORD was upon me, and brought me thither.
> 2   In the visions of God brought he me into the land of Israel . . . .

Ezekiel sounds a lot like me, doesn't he, giving all those dates and times (or I sound a lot like him). People ask me how I remember all the dates and times I refer to in my preaching and teaching.

I'll tell you exactly how it happens. When I mention something that happened in the past, the date or time rises up out of my spirit — out of the inside of me — to my mind, and I know immediately. I'm just following Ezekiel the prophet in giving dates and times! That ability goes along with the prophet's ministry.

In the 33rd chapter of Ezekiel we find something else very interesting:

> **EZEKIEL 33:22**
> 22 Now THE HAND OF THE LORD was upon me in the

evening, afore [before] he that was escaped came: and had
opened my mouth, until he came to me in the morning; and
my mouth was opened, and I was no more dumb.

That means that the hand of the Lord wasn't upon the
prophet in the morning or at midday. The hand of the Lord
was upon him the evening before someone escaped and
came to see him. The prophet went around all night with
his mouth open, never saying a word. He was mute (speechless) until that fellow came. Only then could he speak.

Signs and Wonders

Sister Maria Woodworth-Etter was an early-day Pentecostal preacher whose books I have read. I have some of
her earlier ones. (Only *Signs and Wonders* is now in print.)

Years ago, Sister Etter was preaching in a tent meeting
in St. Louis, Missouri, and the hand of the Lord came upon
her. She had her hand up and her mouth open, about to
say something, when the hand of the Lord fell. She stood
there three days and nights, neither moving nor uttering
a word.

The St. Louis newspapers reported that an estimated
20,000 people filed by to see her. When the anointing of
the Spirit of God lifted from her, her hand went down, her
mouth moved, and she picked up right in the middle of
the sentence she had been preaching three nights before.
(All of her physical senses and functions had been suspended for those three days and nights.)

God used that as a sign.

Did you ever wonder about the verse in Acts that says,
*"And fear came upon every soul: and many wonders and
signs were done by the apostles"* (Acts 2:43)?

I've read many periodicals from Pentecostal people. Some of those early-day ministers had experiences similar to Ezekiel's and Sister Etter's. One fellow told of standing under the power with his mouth open for one day, and others told of being like that all night long.

You might ask, "Why does God do things like that? Why did the hand of the Lord come upon Ezekiel and open his mouth in the evening?" We don't tell God what to do. That's where we miss it.

John the Baptist's father, Zacharias, who was a priest, didn't believe the angel Gabriel's message that a son was to be born to him and his wife. He became speechless and *remained* speechless until John was born (Luke 1). Zacharias wasn't mute from sickness or disease; it was because the hand of the Lord was upon him.

Another example is the "blindness" of Elymas, the sorcerer who withstood Paul on one of his missionary journeys. Paul said, *"And now, behold, the hand of the Lord is upon thee, and thou shalt be blind, not seeing the sun for a season"* (Acts 13:11).

Elymas wasn't struck with disease, for the Spirit of God never has struck anybody with disease. He doesn't have any! Elymas was blind because of the power of God that had come on him.

I've seen things like that happen under my own ministry, and I'm thoroughly convinced that as we learn how to cooperate better with the Spirit of God, there will be even greater manifestations of these things in the last days.

Struck Speechless by the Spirit

Sometimes when I'm preaching, the Spirit of God

comes on me, arrests my attention, and I can't say a word in English. I can speak in tongues, but I can't speak in English (I've tried to.) I can think in English, but I can't say a single word in English — I just absolutely can't. I've been that way sometimes for several hours.

It happened in a great way at our 1981 Campmeeting. I simply couldn't speak in English. The longest time was at Fred Price's church in Inglewood, California, the following month, August 1981.

I had finished my sermon and was laying hands on the sick when suddenly that anointing came on me, and I could not say one word in English.

I turned around and said in tongues to Fred (for I could speak in tongues, but not in English), "You go ahead and lay hands on the people and finish the healing line."

Fred understood me as if I had spoken to him in English. He said to me in tongues — and I heard it as if he were speaking in English, although everybody else heard it in tongues — "All right, you lay your finger in my hands that I may minister with the same anointing, and I will pray for them." I did so, he began to minister, and it seemed as if there were a stronger surge of power than before. I stood there and watched the whole thing, but still couldn't speak in English.

After the service, we went to Fred's home to fellowship and eat. I would start to say something, and I'd say it in tongues. When we were ready to eat, I still couldn't talk to Fred and his family. I began wondering if I'd ever get back to where I could communicate in English again.

When I first came back over into English at Fred Price's home an hour and a half later, I could only speak a word or two. I still couldn't even put sentences together.

Many times when I'm preaching or teaching and the anointing is stronger, a tiny manifestation of this occurs. It's not a matter of what I want to do — I cannot speak in English. I can *think* in English, but I *speak* in tongues. That comes out of your spirit.

As a teenager, I had been paralyzed and bedfast. My tongue became paralyzed and my throat partially paralyzed. Only the people who spent time around me could understand me. When the Holy Spirit is on me so strongly, it's almost that same feeling, except it's not a matter of paralysis.

What is the purpose of becoming speechless? Well, what purpose was there for the Holy Spirit's coming upon Ezekiel in the evening, opening his mouth, and making him remain that way all night until the man came in the morning? The Bible doesn't tell us what the purpose was.

Personally, I think such things often are a sign, and often they prepare you for something.

I think there are aspects of the anointing we are going to come into in the days ahead that we haven't experienced yet. By this I mean the use of the anointing, the purpose of the anointing, the utilization of the anointing, ministering under the anointing, and transferring or transmitting the anointing — on the one hand to do good and bring blessing, and on the other hand to bring judgment on those like Elymas who would stand in the way and hinder the Gospel.

The Ministry of the Seer

The prophet is sometimes called a "seer" in Scripture. Seers see and know things. I used to operate in this more when I stayed in people's homes as we traveled.

In fact, I've never stayed in anybody's home yet without God's warning me about any impending tragedy. If there were going to be a death in the family within the next two years, He'd tell me. Sometimes you can change it and sometimes you can't; He just gets you ready for it.

Years ago I was preaching for friends in California, and on the last night of the meeting, they got some distressing news. Their 16-year-old granddaughter, who had been visiting her other grandparents in Oregon, got on a bus in Portland but wasn't on the bus when it arrived in Los Angeles.

Finally the bus company traced her to Reno, Nevada, but there they lost track of her. Her grandmother burst into tears and was inconsolable. She was sure she would never see this granddaughter again. It was heart-rending.

My wife and I were trying to comfort her. I was sitting in a chair within three feet of her. With my eyes wide open, suddenly I saw myself standing in front of the bus station in Reno. I've never been there, but I know exactly what it looks like. I saw it.

I was standing behind a bus. I saw another bus pull up. It said "Los Angeles" on the front of it. I saw people getting off, including this blonde girl. I saw the other passengers come back, but the girl got on the bus in front of her bus.

I said, "Sister, Sister, Sister — she got on the wrong bus!"

She asked, "Are you sure?"

I said, "Yes, I saw her. She got on the wrong bus."

She asked again, "Are you sure?"

I said, "I'd stake my life on it before I'd say it isn't

so. I'd stake 25 years of ministry on it."

Sure enough, by the time the service was over, a representative of the bus company called and said, "We located your granddaughter in Salt Lake City. She got on the wrong bus. She'll be back in here at 4 o'clock in the morning."

Thank God, the Spirit of God knows.

If I never get any other reward than to have seen that grandmother smile through her tears, that was enough.

Chapter 10
The Anointing of the Apostle

The most significant statement in the Bible regarding this office is that it was filled by Christ Himself, as we saw in Chapter 1.

The Greek word *apostolos*, translated "apostle," means "one sent forth, a sent one." Jesus Christ is the greatest example of a sent one:

> JOHN 20:21
> 21 Then said Jesus to them again, Peace be unto you: AS MY FATHER HATH SENT ME, even so send I you.

A true apostle is always one with a commission — not one who merely goes, but one who is *sent*. A Bible example is found in Acts 13, where Barnabas and Paul were sent forth to be apostles to the Gentiles.

The Bible also speaks of the signs of an apostle:

> 2 CORINTHIANS 12:12
> 12 Truly the signs of an APOSTLE were wrought among you in all patience, in signs, and wonders, and mighty deeds.

The "signs," then, are signs, wonders, and mighty deeds.

To stand in this office, one must have a personal experience with the Lord — something very deep and real, something beyond the ordinary — not just something secondhand or handed down by tradition.

Notice that Paul said, in defending his apostleship, *"Am I not an apostle? am I not free? HAVE I NOT SEEN JESUS CHRIST OUR LORD?..."* (1 Cor. 9:1).

Paul did not see Jesus in the flesh as the twelve did,

but he saw Jesus in a spiritual vision (Acts 9:3-6). He had a deep spiritual experience with the Lord. Even his conversion was beyond the ordinary.

In fact, Paul had such a deep spiritual experience with the Lord that he could say concerning what he knew about the Lord's Supper, *"For I have received of the Lord that which also I delivered unto you . . . . "* (1 Cor. 11:23). Paul didn't learn what he knew about this subject from the other apostles. He got it by revelation. Jesus gave it to him.

Paul wasn't taught the Gospel he preached by man. The Spirit of God taught it to him. He wrote, *"But I certify you, brethren, that the gospel which was preached of me is not after man. For I neither received it of man, neither was I taught it, but by the revelation of Jesus Christ"* (Gal. 1:11,12).

The work of an apostle is that of a foundation layer:

1 CORINTHIANS 3:10
10 According to the grace of God which is given unto me, as a wise masterbuilder, I HAVE LAID THE FOUNDATION, and another buildeth thereon. But let every man take heed how he buildeth thereupon.

EPHESIANS 2:20
20 And are built upon THE FOUNDATION OF THE APOSTLES and prophets, Jesus Christ himself being the chief corner stone.

The first twelve apostles laid the foundation of the Church as the earliest pioneers and preachers of the Gospel. They also laid the foundation of the Church by receiving the Holy Spirit.

An apostle's ministry seems to embrace all other

ministry gifts. The distinguishing result is *the ability to establish churches.*

The apostle has the supernatural equipment called "governments" listed in First Corinthians 12:28. (Weymouth translates it "powers of organization.")

After churches are established, apostles can exercise authority over those churches they have established (1 Cor. 9:1,2).

There are many who call themselves apostles who want to dominate and rule people. They say, "I'm an apostle. I have authority. You have to do what I say."

In New Testament days, the apostles could exercise authority only over the churches they had established themselves. Paul, for example, never exercised any authority over the church at Jerusalem, or any of the churches other apostles had established.

Remember, these offices are in *power* and not in *name.* If the power is not there to establish churches, then those involved are not apostles.

A missionary who is really called of God and sent by the Holy Spirit is an apostle.

In Acts 13:2, the Holy Spirit said, *"Separate me Barnabas and Saul* [Paul] *for the work whereunto I have called them."* Verse 4 continues, *"So they, being SENT FORTH by the Holy Ghost, departed . . . . "* They were "sent ones." They left on their first missionary journey to the Gentiles.

The New Testament never mentions missionaries, yet that is an important office. It is here in the office of apostle.

A missionary will have the ability of all the ministry gifts:

He will do the work of the *evangelist.* He will get people saved. He will do the work of the *teacher.* He will teach and establish people. He will do the work of the *pastor*. He will pastor and shepherd people for a while.

In studying closely the life of the Apostle Paul, we note that he said he never built on a foundation someone else had laid. He endeavored to preach the Gospel where Christ was not named (Rom. 15:20), and he always stayed in a place from six months to three years.

His real calling was not to be a pastor, but he stayed long enough to get his converts established in the truth before moving on.

Some wonder if there are apostles today. No one, not even Paul, could be an apostle in the sense the original twelve were. There are only "twelve apostles of the Lamb" (Rev. 21:14).

Their qualifications were outlined in Acts 1, when the twelve selected an apostle to take Judas' place. We see from verses 21 and 22 that to be one of the twelve apostles of the Lamb, one had to have accompanied the apostles and Jesus during the entire time of His 3½-year ministry (Paul was not with them).

Also, the original twelve were "sent ones" to be eye-witnesses of the ministry, works, life, death, burial, resurrection, and ascension of the Lord Jesus Christ. They stood in a place no other apostles or ministries can ever stand.

There are, however, apostles today in the sense that Barnabas, Paul, and others were apostles.

We have seen listed in Ephesians 4:11, *"And he gave some, APOSTLES...."* If God has taken this or any other ministry out of this list, then the Bible should have told us that He gave them for just a little while.

All of the ministry gifts were given for the perfecting of the saints, the work of the ministry, and the edifying of the Body of Christ. This includes apostles. Thank God, the office of the apostle exists today!

For how long did God give the ministry gifts? According to verse 13, *all* of them were given *"Till we all come in the unity of the faith, and of the knowledge of the Son of God, unto a perfect man, unto the measure of the stature of the fulness of Christ."*

In summary, the four marks we look for in an apostle today are:

1. Outstanding spiritual gifts.
2. Deep personal experience.
3. Power and ability to establish churches.
4. Ability to provide adequate spiritual leadership.

If you think God called you to be an apostle, don't bother about it. You won't start out there anyway. Paul didn't. Acts 13:1 says, *"Now there were in the church that was at Antioch certain PROPHETS AND TEACHERS; as Barnabas, and Simeon . . . and Lucius . . . and Manaen . . . and Saul."*

Each of these men was either a prophet *or* a teacher, or a prophet *and* a teacher. Some may operate in more than one office — but a person doesn't operate in those offices as he wills. It is as God wills and as He anoints.

Barnabas was a teacher. Saul (Paul) was a prophet and a teacher, for a prophet is one who has visions and revelations, and Paul received the entire Gospel that way. He would have been called a "seer" in the Old Testament, because he would see and know things supernaturally.

As we have seen, in Acts 13:2 the Holy Spirit said, *"Separate me Barnabas and Saul for the work whereunto I have called them."* They had not yet gotten into the work that God called them to do. They fasted and prayed again, and the other ministers laid hands on them and sent them out, and they became apostles or missionaries to the Gentiles.

Barnabas was considered an apostle as much as Paul was: *"Which when the APOSTLES, Barnabas and Paul...."* (Acts 14:14).

In the city of Lystra, during this first missionary voyage, Paul ministered healing to a man who had been crippled from birth (Acts 14:8), and the people of the city wanted to worship Paul and Barnabas as gods, saying, *"The gods are come down to us in the likeness of men"* (v. 11). Paul and Barnabas had moved into another office, that of apostle, and a stronger anointing had come, because it takes a stronger anointing to stand in that office.

Don't get taken up with names and titles. If I didn't know what God called me to, I wouldn't bother a minute about it. If I sensed the call on the inside of me, I would just preach and teach and let God eventually set me in the office He has for me.

Notice Barnabas and Paul were not set in the office of apostle to begin with, but God eventually did set them there.

Also remember this: God rewards *faithfulness*. He doesn't reward *offices*. A prophet won't receive any more reward than a janitor who was faithful in his ministry of helps.

Higher offices do not receive greater rewards; there is just a greater responsibility.

(For an in-depth study of the fivefold ministries and the other ministry gifts, read my study guide, *The Ministry Gifts.*)

Chapter 11
How To Increase the Anointing

There is an anointing on you, whether you recognize it or not, if you're called to any office or ministry.

And no matter which office you stand in, or what you are called to do, you can have something to do with determining the *degree* of your anointing. You can prepare yourself for this anointing. If it doesn't come on you, it's because you didn't prepare yourself.

Furthermore, the anointing can be increased. You can *increase* the anointing by studying the Word and by being prayerful.

You can *decrease* the anointing by neglecting to study and pray.

A workman who doesn't study (2 Tim. 2:15) is going to be ashamed, because people are going to find out about it, and he'll either lose the anointing, or the anointing will not be in manifestation. If you do your part, however, this will not happen.

If you'll study and pray, when you get up and start out in faith, the anointing will come. When I used to preach under that preaching anointing, most of the time I'd have to start out in faith — I didn't particularly feel anything — but that anointing never failed to come on me to preach. (And sometimes it will linger on and you will enjoy it, praise God.)

You have to realize that one standing in the office of the prophet, the pastor, the evangelist, or whatever can be more or less anointed.

I think it's quite obvious as you listen to different ministers that sometimes they are more anointed than at other times. Sometimes teachers are more anointed to teach than they are at other times. Sometimes the prophet is more anointed than he is at other times. There are areas and degrees of anointings.

In Old Testament times, the Holy Spirit came *upon* three types of people — the *prophet,* the *priest,* and the *king* — to enable them to function in their respective offices. But the Holy Spirit wasn't *in* any of them during that dispensation as He is in ours.

Did you know that David was anointed to be *king* of Israel, but he also was a *prophet?* The anointing of the prophet was upon him.

Remember those two prophets in the Old Testament, Elijah and his successor, Elisha? Elisha asked for — and received — a "double portion" of Elijah's anointing. That doesn't mean there are two Holy Spirits — there is just one.

What Elisha called a "double portion" we could term a "double measure" of the anointing to stand in the same office. Such a measure of anointing would not be available to someone not called to that office. They wouldn't need it. (For example, if you're called to be a pastor, you don't need the prophet's anointing. Elisha was called to the office of prophet, however.)

How To Get a Mantle

When I was among the Baptists, we didn't hear much about the mantle falling on anybody. I don't think the mantle was on many of us. But when I got over in Full Gospel circles, I heard quite a bit about it, because they know so much more about the anointing.

I can tell preachers how to get the mantle of any

ministry they want, because you can see the answers right here in the story of Elijah and Elisha.

> **1 KINGS 19:19**
> 19 So he departed thence, and found Elisha the son of Shaphat, who was plowing with twelve yoke of oxen before him, and he with the twelfth: and Elijah passed by him, and CAST HIS MANTLE UPON HIM.

This mantle actually was a symbol of that particular office. It *stood for* the anointing of the Holy Spirit. It showed that the Holy Spirit was coming upon Elisha, but it wasn't the actual anointing itself. It is a symbol of the Holy Spirit and the power of God.

The mantle will envelop an individual and he or she will minister under the anointing that goes with whatever their office or calling of God is.

The word "mantle" means a cloak. Sometimes in ministry, when the anointing comes on me, it *seems* like a cloak is coming down over me. It feels like I might be wearing an overcoat — yet I'm really not. But the power of God — the anointing — so envelops me that I'll feel that way.

> **1 KINGS 19:20**
> 20 And he [Elisha] left the oxen, and ran after Elijah, and said, Let me, I pray thee, kiss my father and my mother, and then I will follow thee. And he said unto him, Go back again: for what have I done to thee?

Elijah was saying, "Just go on back and forget it." In other words, "If you're going to put other things first, no matter how legitimate they may be, you're not going to enjoy the fullness of God's anointing."

Elisha didn't go back and kiss his parents goodbye.
He took a yoke of oxen, killed and cooked them, and fed
them to the people. *"Then he arose, and went after Elijah,
and ministered unto him,"* verse 21 says.

> **2 KINGS 2:1,2**
> 1   And it came to pass, when the Lord would take up Elijah
> into heaven by a whirlwind, that Elijah went with Elisha
> from Gilgal.
> 2   And Elijah said unto Elisha, Tarry here, I pray thee;
> for the Lord hath sent me to Bethel. And Elisha said unto
> him, As the Lord liveth, and as thy soul liveth, I will not
> leave thee. So they went down to Bethel.

Notice how closely Elisha followed Elijah. Elijah even
tried to convince him to wait behind. I think the Lord tries
people sometimes purposely. Through Elijah, He tried
Elisha. He wanted to be sure that Elisha was made of the
right stuff before this anointing came on him. Elisha
replied, *"As the Lord liveth . . . I will not leave thee."*

Finally Elisha arrived at the place where he could get
what he wanted. Elijah said, *"Ask what I shall do for thee,
before I be taken away from thee."* And Elisha responded,
*"I pray thee, let A DOUBLE PORTION OF THY SPIRIT
BE UPON ME"* (v. 9).

What he meant was he wanted a double portion of that
anointing of God to stand in the office of prophet. God
anoints men and women to stand in certain offices. And
some can be more anointed than others.

Elijah said, *"Thou hast asked a hard thing: never-
theless, if thou see me when I am taken from thee, it shall
be so unto thee . . . ."* (v. 10).

2 KINGS 2:11-13
11 And it came to pass, as they still went on, and talked,
that, behold, there appeared a chariot of fire, and horses
of fire, and parted them both asunder; and Elijah went up
by a whirlwind into heaven.
12 And Elisha saw it, and he cried, My father, my father,
the chariot of Israel, and the horsemen thereof. And he saw
him [Elijah] no more: and he took hold of his own clothes,
and rent them in two pieces.
13 He took up also the mantle of Elijah that fell from him,
and went back, and stood by the bank of Jordan.

Elisha stayed right with Elijah and was with him when
he was taken. Notice that before Elisha took up Elijah's
mantle, he took off his own clothes and tore them in half.
Then he picked up that mantle and put it on, for *that
mantle covered a person's whole being.*

Reading on through the Old Testament, you'll find that
usually the mantle they wore was really the skin of an
animal. Over in the New Testament it speaks about John
the Baptist and his dress. It says that John the Baptist
was hairy. That doesn't mean he was physically so; it
means he wore one of these coats of skin.

The story continues in the next two verses:

2 KINGS 2:14,15
14 And he took the mantle of Elijah that fell from him,
and smote the waters, and said, Where is the Lord God of
Elijah? and when he also had smitten the waters, they
parted hither and thither: and Elisha went over.
15 And when the sons of the prophets which were to view
at Jericho saw him, they said, The spirit of Elijah doth rest
on Elisha. And they came to meet him, and bowed themselves to the ground before him.

It wasn't just the mantle — the hairy coat — that

divided the waters; if it had been, everyone could have parted waters, because they all wore skin coats — *it was the anointing that did it.* That's why the sons of the prophets said, *"The spirit of Elijah doth rest on Elisha."*

So Elisha did see Elijah caught up into heaven and he did get a double portion of the anointing to stand in the office of prophet. And if you'll read the Bible account of his ministry, it's recorded that he did twice as many miracles as Elijah.

By studying his story, we learn something about getting the anointing. Elisha stayed right with Elijah. He didn't let the prophet out of his sight. *He followed him closely.* The same spirit got hold of him.

You see, *that same anointing — or that same spirit — will come by* ASSOCIATION, ENVIRONMENT, *and* INFLUENCE.

Did you ever notice that those who work closely with me have the same anointing on them that I have on me? In fact, there are some anointings in some ministries that have left me — I don't even have them anymore. My workers got them! That's absolutely the truth. But that's the way you get anointings.

Smith Wigglesworth's Mantle

Frequently when some great man or woman of God passes off the scene, like Elijah did, you will hear preachers say, "I wonder upon whom his mantle will fall?" We've all heard that said. But just because we've heard something said and have repeated it often doesn't make it so! Something isn't so just because we thought it was so.

I want you to see something here that can hinder you

from entering into the blessings God wants you to have.

In 1947, I picked up a religious periodical and read that Smith Wigglesworth had gone to be with the Lord at age 87. I felt a great loss. I remember I went into my church and fell across the altar. I didn't know the man personally, but I had read about him constantly, actually wearing his books out, until something from him rubbed off on me.

You feel an emptiness — a vacuum — when a man of God of that caliber leaves — a man who had had 23 people raised from the dead in his ministry.

People asked, "I wonder on whom his mantle will fall?" In my ignorance, I, too, thought that the *mantle* is the *anointing,* and it would fall *at random* on somebody.

But that's not correct. The mantle symbolizes the anointing. Furthermore, *the mantle is not decreed to fall upon some particular individual* — and it doesn't. The mantle doesn't even come to you that way!

How, then, did Elisha get Elijah's mantle and a double portion of the prophet's anointing? *He followed Elijah closely.* As we saw earlier, you get the same anointing by *association, environment,* and *influence.*

No doubt you'll be led of the Lord to follow certain ministries, but there are certain things that ministers need to be warned about in this regard. I'm in my 49th year of ministry. You stumble upon a few things in 49 years.

If you are going to follow somebody, be sure they are following the Lord. If they get off a little — just a little — don't follow that. Learn faith from them, but don't follow them too closely.

Remember these three things:

First, have the call of God on your life.

Second, follow the Lord Jesus — He's the Head of the

Church — very, very closely.

Third, if you want the same type of ministry someone else has, follow that ministry closely. If the desire for it is in your heart, it's usually because God put it there. But that mantle will not fall on you automatically, like ripe cherries off a tree.

In the days of the Voice of Healing organization, which flourished during the great Healing Revival, I watched some of those ministries. God sent me to some ministers to tell them not to do certain things — but they went ahead and did them anyway.

They started following a certain person, and then that person missed it — and I saw his followers miss it the same way. I saw this happen to several men. Some of them died at exactly the same age that the man they were following had died. You see, they followed him too closely. You might learn something from them.

It's like something I heard P.C. "Dad" Nelson, the founder of Southwestern Assemblies of God College, say in the spring before he went home to be with the Lord. (He died in the fall of 1942 at age 74.)

Dad Nelson was talking about John Alexander Dowie, a Congregational minister who had a healing ministry long before all of ours. Dowie got a revelation of divine healing from Acts 10:38 while pastoring down in Australia. Later he came to the United States, settling in Chicago. He founded Zion, Illinois, as a Christian city. Gordon Lindsay was born there. Dowie laid hands on him when he was a baby.

Brother Lindsay, who headed the Voice of Healing and founded Christ for the Nations, got some copies of Dowie's publication, *Leaves of Healing,* and published some of his sermons. Brother Lindsay also wrote Dowie's outstanding biography, *The Life of John Alexander Dowie.*

The incident Dad Nelson related concerning Dowie had to have happened before 1907, because Dowie died in 1907 at age 60. Dad Nelson was still a Baptist pastor at the time of the story (he didn't get the baptism with the Holy Spirit and enter the healing ministry himself until 1921).

Dad Nelson said, "I saw Dowie in the presence of six of us denominational ministers and five medical doctors. The doctors had brought in a woman who had a malignant growth on the side of her face.

"It looked like a giant eggplant — blue-purplish — and it grew inside her mouth and covered the whole side of her face. It was almost as big as her head. Doctors couldn't treat it, it was so big. In those days what they would have treated it with was poisonous, and the woman might have absorbed too much of the poison.

"I saw Dowie, in the presence of six of us denominational ministers and five medical doctors take hold of that malignant growth, say, 'In the Name of the Lord Jesus Christ!' — and strip it off of her face. The doctors examined her face immediately and said, 'That's baby skin. That's newborn skin on the whole side of her face.' "

Then Dad Nelson added, *"You can follow Dowie's faith, but you can't follow his doctrine!"*

In his latter years, Dowie had missed God.

Some will ask, "Can you be wrong in *doctrine* and strong in *faith?* " Certainly. We've seen that in the lives of Dowie and others. You need to realize that a person can be right in his heart and wrong in his head!

That's why you need to be careful about whom you follow — especially in the ministry. A young man who follows another man closely will make the same mistakes the older fellow got into. Learn something from him if you can, but like Dad Nelson said, "You can follow his faith, but you can't follow his doctrine."

More than once I've seen people in marvelous, legitimate ministries get off. And I've seen the same thing happen with the pastoral office. Of course, people are always talking about somebody who failed. (I like to follow somebody, bless God, who didn't fail!)

Knowing you believe in divine healing, somebody will say, "Now, Brother So-and-so had a healing ministry, and he died at an early age, and then Brother So-and-so died, too."

I always say, "I don't know why he died. That's not my problem or any of my business. I'm not his lord and master. That's between him and the Lord. I'm not following him anyway; I'm following the Lord."

But if I wanted to follow somebody's example, I'd take Smith Wigglesworth. He lived his life out, praise God, and died without sickness at 87.

Another good example was a minister who was a Baptist until he got baptized with the Holy Spirit, spoke with other tongues, and preached divine healing.

I had heard a number of rumors concerning his death, but then I visited his daughter while holding meetings in her state. I came to find out that when this gentleman was 93, he announced at the breakfast table one morning, "It's time for me to go home."

His daughter and wife (who was considerably younger than he) decided he must be getting senile and didn't realize he already *was* at home.

His daughter told me, "Momma and I finished the

dishes and went into the sitting room. He was sitting there in the chair and said, 'I told you all I'm going home today. There's Jesus — goodbye!' "

Sitting in the rocker, he took off. I believe I'll follow him closely, hallelujah!

Remember what Paul said:

1 CORINTHIANS 11:1
1 Be ye followers of me, even as I also am of Christ.

It's all right to follow people as long as they are following Christ closely.

Chapter 12
Yielding to the Anointing

I'm convinced that the more we yield to the Spirit of God and are taken over by Him, the more results we would see.

Demons take people over against their will and manifest themselves through them, but the Spirit of God will not do that against your will.

Why can't we be more yielded to the Spirit of God? I know one reason for me is that I get over into that realm sometimes and get afraid. It's not like a fear of snakes or cyclones; it's a holy fear, a holy awe. I get over into that realm and get afraid I can't get back.

I think that's what happened to Enoch: He got over there so far he just went on over, body and all!

I don't know about your experience, but moving in the realm of the supernatural — stepping out of the natural — is not the easiest thing to do. However, if we'll learn to yield to the anointing and not be afraid, mighty things will happen.

One man who learned to do this was Smith Wigglesworth.

I never heard Smith Wigglesworth minister. If I'd have known about it, I could have, because he was in Dallas in 1937 while on his last trip to the United States. That was the year I received the baptism in the Holy Spirit, and I lived just 32 miles away, but I didn't know he was there in Dallas for three night services at the First Assembly of God Church.

I quote from his writings frequently. Someone once asked me concerning his book *Ever Increasing Faith*, "Do you understand that?"

"Yes, I understand it," I said. "He speaks my language!"

One pastor said, "I've read that book five times, and I haven't understood what he's talking about yet."

It's difficult to understand if you're not over there in that realm.

An elderly minister in California told me of hearing Wigglesworth preach in Southern California. He said, "Sometimes when he started out, he just wouldn't make sense. He stumbled around. Then the Spirit of God would come on him. It would startle the congregation. You could see it. His countenance would change, and the words would just flow out of his mouth. It looked like he'd turned into another man."

Wigglesworth went to work in a factory when he was 6 years old. They didn't have child labor laws in England then, so he never went to school a day in his life. His wife taught him to read.

I remember Donald Gee, one of the leaders of the Assemblies of God movement in Great Britain. I heard him preach when he was in the United States in 1939. He spoke of Wigglesworth.

Wigglesworth didn't belong to any particular Pentecostal group; he preached for all of them.

Brother Gee said, "We would always have Brother Wigglesworth preach every year at our general conference. We wanted to expose our young ministers to his prophetic anointing so they could learn how to yield to the Spirit of God."

Wigglesworth spoke for them in 1947, just a few weeks before he went home to be with the Lord at age 87. He spoke of Romans 8:11, *"But if the Spirit of him that raised up Jesus from the dead dwell in you, he that raised up Christ from the dead shall also quicken* [He'll quicken, quicken, quicken] *your mortal bodies by his Spirit that dwelleth in you.*"

I think there's something over in this area that we'll lose if we're not careful. The old-time Pentecostals would pray until they got the unction or anointing to deliver a message. I think they had something we don't realize sometimes.

We say, "We're people of faith. We'll just start out."

That's good only if you have made the right preparation.

Chapter 13
Peculiar Anointings

If we're not careful, those of us in what is called the "faith ministry" get rather spoiled, wanting only one type of ministry. We need all types of ministry. We need to learn to appreciate all types of ministry.

Pastors need to expose their people to all types of ministries, realizing that God uses people where they are, and recognizing and appreciating the anointing that is upon them.

I'm convinced God is going to use some people in peculiar ways in these days, but they first must be sure the unction or anointing is there. If it gets the job done, praise God for it. That's what counts. Recognize it and praise God for it, wherever it is.

When I first came into Full Gospel circles, a man with a peculiar anointing came to our church. I had never seen anything like his ministry. Because it didn't "fit" me, I was disgusted.

The first time I saw him, I thought, *Oh, my!* I hid my face, I was so embarrassed. I said, "O dear God, it's time to give the altar service, and here the man's dancing. Nobody will get saved!"

Yet when he gave the altar call, people started coming down every aisle to get saved. I sat there and wept, saying, "Lord, forgive me. O my God, forgive me!"

When I became a pastor, I invited Old Dad Smith to hold me a meeting in every church I ever pastored but one. As a matter of fact, I wasn't in a church very long before I would have him come.

This fellow was strictly an evangelist. He just preached the Good News that Jesus saves. That's about as far as he went.

Do you know what his anointing was? He'd dance people to the altar. *Old Dad Smith would give an altar call dancing!*

When I first saw him, he was 63 years old. He held me a meeting when he was over 70, too.

My first impression was, *Well, he might reach a few uneducated folks.* But he reached educated people! Lawyers, bankers, doctors, and judges would get saved, and in one place the mayor of the town got saved. He danced them down to the altar. The anointing was upon him. You could see it when it came upon him.

Yet he'd start out in the natural. He'd say to his daughter, "Inez, strike up a tune." Inez would strike up a tune, and he'd start dancing in the flesh. He might dance that way for a little while, but then you could see it: The Spirit of God would hit him. The anointing would come on him. It was so phenomenal the crowd could see it, too. Sinners would gasp. They could see that something had come on him suddenly.

It was light. It was powerful. It was a blessing. It would draw people to the altar.

(There is a secret involved here: Dad Smith would start out dancing in the flesh and *then* the anointing would hit him.)

I didn't attempt to imitate him, however. If you go out and start doing something just because somebody else is doing it, it won't work for you.

God said He would take the foolish things to confound the wise. If God wanted to use him that way, what business was it of mine? He got results.

Now, Dad Smith didn't know a thing in the world about

faith, but that was all right. He was getting more people saved than I was, and I could teach his converts faith *after* he got them into the kingdom. That wasn't his ministry anyway. His ministry was getting people saved.

He could have revivals when nobody else could. He could get people saved when nobody else could. Back then if you got half a dozen saved and three baptized with the Holy Spirit, you thought you had a landslide. Dad Smith always would have more results than that.

I'll tell you, we don't need to turn our noses up at anything God's doing. If it's bringing blessing to people and getting them saved and baptized with the Holy Spirit, thank God for it.

I read in the Old Testament where God used a donkey once. I always get great blessings from that. I think, *If He could use a donkey, He surely could use me!*

Let God use you the way He wants to. Quit trying to be like somebody else.

Special Anointings

God will anoint you for whatever He has called you to do, but He anoints some people to minister in special ways, too. Some of us are anointed with *special anointings,* and such anointings on ministries bring forth marvelous results.

I'm bringing this up because I believe some extraordinary things are going to happen before long. I want to prepare you for them so you won't miss them or draw back from them simply because you haven't seen anything like them before. I want you to be ready to move with God.

One New Testament example concerns the Apostle Paul:

> ACTS 19:11,12
> 11 And God wrought SPECIAL MIRACLES by the hands
> of Paul:
> 12 So that from his body were brought unto the sick
> handkerchiefs or aprons, and the diseases departed from
> them, and the evil spirits went out of them.

We saw that Jesus was anointed by the Holy Spirit to stand in the fivefold ministry offices.

He also was anointed to minister healing. When the woman with the issue of blood touched Him, power went out of Him — power that He was anointed with. What kind of power was it? Healing power.

But Jesus didn't always just lay hands on people, and people didn't always touch Him. He ministered to people in various ways.

One time He spat on the ground, made clay of the spittle, rubbed it on a blind man's eyes, and said, *"Go, wash in the pool of Siloam . . . He went his way therefore, and washed, and came seeing"* (John 9:7).

Do you think Jesus did that because He laid awake nights trying His best to think up something different? No, He was suddenly anointed by the Spirit of God. God will use people in different ways.

On another occasion they brought a man who was deaf and had a speech impediment to Jesus. The Bible says Jesus put His fingers into the man's ears, spat, and touched his tongue. *"And straightway his ears were opened, and the string of his tongue was loosed, and he spake plain"* (Mark 7:35).

Why do you think Jesus did that to him? Did He think, *Well, I spat on the ground and rubbed it on the blind man's eyes. I'll try it here and see if it works?* No, He didn't make a practice of that; there aren't that many references to it. Still, I'm sure He did it more often than the Word of God tells us, because *the anointing was there to do it.* And when it's done under the anointing, it works.

The Bible only tells us a little of what Jesus did. John said, *"And there are also many other things which Jesus did, the which, if they should be written every one, I suppose that even the world itself could not contain the books that should be written"* (John 21:25).

I don't minister in all the ways that Jesus ministered; I never spit on anybody! Yet somebody might minister that way and that might be the only way they'd minister, because their anointing is there.

One of the founding fathers of the Assemblies of God movement told me personally of such a case while we were talking along these lines.

He said, "In the early days of the Assemblies of God movement, there was a minister I knew personally who did this and I've never seen anybody who had the success that this man had — none of them! I was in Wigglesworth's meetings; I was in Raymond T. Richie's meetings; I was in Charles S. Price's meetings; I was in Sister Aimee Semple McPherson's meetings; I was in all of the Voice of Healing meetings — but I've never seen anybody who had his success.

"Of course, he didn't minister to the multitudes; he was a country fellow, a farmer who had gotten saved. He never preached anywhere but out in the country in country school houses. Back in those days the country was full of people.

He continued, "Very seldom would a person fail to get healed in his meetings. I was standing right by his side, and he'd always spit on them — every single one of them. He'd spit in his hand and rub it on them. That's the way he ministered."

He said, "They brought a fellow up to him once — I was standing only five feet away — and he was a grown man, 40-some years old. His left arm was just like any other person's, but his right arm was a little ol' arm just eight inches long hanging off his shoulder. That man spit in his hand and rubbed it on that arm and I saw it grow right out the same length as the other and the hand grow the same size as the other."

This brother said, "If something was wrong with your head, he'd spit in his hand and rub it on your forehead. If you had stomach trouble, he'd spit in his hand and rub it on your clothes and on your stomach. If you had something wrong with your knee, he'd spit in his hand and rub it on your knee. And all the people would get healed. Why? God told him to."

You can't argue with success. None of us minister in all the ways Jesus ministered, because we don't stand in all of those offices, but we may minister in some ways He ministered.

Several times the anointing has come on me to do unusual things while praying for the sick. Sometimes I go along five or six years between times.

The first time it happened to me was in 1950. I was preaching in Oklahoma. A woman came forward for prayer. She said she was 72, but she looked like she was about to give birth to a baby. Of course, she had a tumor.

She had been operated on twice in Oklahoma City, but the tumor had come back the third time, and the doctors wouldn't operate again. They said, "We feel you'll live longer if we don't operate on you anymore. You'll probably live another few years."

She told me, "Eighteen months have passed, and you can see this huge tumor."

"Well," I replied, "isn't it wonderful that we have inside information? Himself took our — and your — infirmities, and bare our — and your — sicknesses. Healing's yours."

"Yes," she said. "That's right. Healing's mine, and I'll be healed, too."

I started to lay hands on her to pray when the Word of the Lord came to me, saying, "Hit her in the stomach with your fist."

On the inside of me, I said, "Lord, You're going to get me in trouble, going around hitting women in the stomach with my fist! I don't believe I much want to do that!"

Well, if you get to arguing about it, the anointing will leave you — it will lift from you just like a bird flying away after sitting on your shoulder. It left me.

When it left me I thought, *Well, I'll go ahead and minister with laying on of hands.* I laid hands on her again and the anointing came again and the Word of the Lord came again: "Hit her in the stomach with your fist."

I decided I had better stop and explain that to the crowd before I started doing it. So I told them what the Lord said, and I punched her in the stomach with my fist. And God and hundreds of people are my witnesses that that stomach went down like you'd stuck a pin in a balloon.

And she gathered her dress up around her and said, "Why — why — why, it's gone!"

I said, "It sure has."

She looked at me sort of startled and said, "I don't

know where it went."

I said, "I don't, either."

Where did it go? Thank God, it just went.

That was my first experience along that line. But I didn't go around hitting people in the stomach with my fist from then on just because I had the unction that one time! Without the unction, nothing would have happened, and I might have gotten into trouble.

Through the years, the Lord has said to me several times, "Hit them." I've never hit anybody yet without their being instantly healed.

Several years ago we were ministering in Atlanta, Georgia, and the Spirit of God led me to call out somebody who was very hard of hearing in one ear. When the man got down to the front, the Spirit of God told me to hit him.

I hit him on the side of the head, and it popped like a gun went off. Some people asked him about it later, and he said, "I have no knowledge of it. It didn't hurt. I thought he tapped me lightly." But his deaf ear was opened.

And then — and I don't know why I said it — I suddenly had the unction to say, "Run down the aisle." He turned and ran down the aisle. He hadn't run in 20 years.

As this man was changing clothes later, preparing to come to the next service, he called to his wife, "Look, look, look!" All of his varicose veins had completely disappeared.

Now, you can't ordinarily get people healed simply by having them run down the aisle, but when the unction's there — when the anointing's there — it works, glory to God!

Not long ago I was teaching in the afternoon at our

Healing School, and just as I came to the close of the service I saw myself hit somebody in the back, right over their right kidney, with my fist. All I saw was the back of the person. Whoever it was was wearing blue jeans, so I thought it was a man.

I spoke that right out: "God wants me to minister to somebody. Your right kidney doesn't function at all and the left one not much, but it's the right one that's failed."

A woman came down front. She had on those blue jeans I had seen. I said, "Now I'm going to do what I saw myself do." I didn't know a thing in the world about her or her condition, but I hit her in the back with my fist right over that kidney.

She was a RHEMA student who was being treated at the City of Faith. Her doctors were very worried about that kidney and had scheduled a biopsy because the kidney wasn't working. But when she told them what God had had me do, her Spirit-filled doctor said, "We'll just wait, then, on the surgery." She never did have the surgery; that kidney started functioning again.

I saw that in the realm of the Spirit. A lot goes along with the anointing of the prophet. Thank God for the anointing.

I believe we're going to see some things over in this area of anointing that we haven't seen before.

A black preacher called it "the ointment." In the Old Testament they talked about the ointment, which was a type of the anointing.

Somebody asked this preacher, "What's that you keep talking about? What is it?"

He said, "Well, I don't know what it *is,* but I know what it *ain't.* " And I concur with him, praise God. We may not know altogether what it *is,* but we know when it *ain't.* And it's quite obvious sometimes, not only in our preaching, but in our singing and our ministering, that it "ain't."

God wants to raise up a mighty spiritual army in these days, equipped with His power and His Spirit, that He can place His anointing upon.

Seek the Lord concerning your own ministry. Are you where He wants you? Have you got the anointing upon you that you should have to stand in that office? Or are you just a hanger-on?

Do you have a desire to do something for God, but you don't know where your place is, and you think, *Well, I'm working for the Lord, so that's fine* ? But it's not fine. Did He call you or not? Is the anointing on you?

Chapter 14
The Healing Anointing

There is a healing anointing.

Jesus said, *"The Spirit of the Lord is upon me, because HE HATH ANOINTED ME to preach the gospel to the poor; he hath sent me TO HEAL...."* (Luke 4:18).

Acts 10:38 also refers to Jesus' anointing to heal: *"How GOD ANOINTED JESUS of Nazareth with the Holy Ghost and with power: WHO WENT ABOUT doing good, and HEALING all that were oppressed of the devil; for God was with him."*

I got people healed after I was saved and had the Holy Spirit dwelling in me. I didn't have the baptism of the Holy Spirit yet — I didn't know about it.

I myself had been healed by acting upon the promises of God, not by being ministered to by somebody who was anointed. I had been healed reading Mark 11:23,24: *"When ye pray, believe that ye receive ... and ye shall have...."* (v. 24).

I taught people what I had learned: that you can be healed through faith and prayer. I knew nothing about ministering with an anointing to heal, although I knew something about preaching with an anointing. When I prayed for people's healing, I never felt anything. Nothing went out of me into them.

The Pentecostals I began associating with knew a depth in the Holy Spirit that I didn't know, and they waited for something supernatural to happen. When it happened, someone got healed, but if it didn't, they didn't know how to teach people to believe God and receive by faith alone.

I just went along ministering by faith, basing healing

on the promises of the Word of God, and getting people healed on a regular basis. (Smith Wigglesworth said, "There's something about believing God that will cause God to pass over a million people just to get to you.")

Even after I was baptized in the Holy Spirit, I still wasn't conscious of any anointing to minister healing. I still ministered to people through faith and prayer, laying hands on them in faith.

I'd been baptized with the Holy Spirit for about two years before I was conscious of an anointing or transfer of power that sometimes would go out of me into other people. We can be conscious of a flow of anointing because the Holy Spirit — the life of God — is in us, and can be ministered to others.

It's a matter of how much faith you have: little faith, little results; more faith, more results. I think that's the reason I had more results than many Pentecostal ministers even before I was baptized in the Holy Spirit.

Any believer — layman or preacher — can lay hands on the sick, because healing belongs to them; it was purchased for them at Calvary. We are authorized to pray — we don't need any special leading — we're already instructed to do so. The Bible says, *"These signs shall follow them that believe ... they shall lay hands on the sick, and they shall recover"* (Mark 16:17,18).

Thus, people today can believe the Word and be healed of anything without any special manifestation of God's miraculous ministry gifts or spiritual gifts. On the other hand, some are anointed with the healing anointing.

How Jesus Ministered Healing

Notice that Jesus ministered healing with an anointing

of healing power. We can learn something about that healing anointing in Mark 5, the story of the woman with the
issue of blood.

> MARK 5:25-34
> 25 And a certain woman, which had an issue of blood
> twelve years,
> 26 And had suffered many things of many physicians, and
> had spent all that she had, and was nothing bettered, but
> rather grew worse,
> 27 When she had heard of Jesus, came in the press behind,
> and touched his garment.
> 28 For she said, If I may touch but his clothes, I shall be
> whole.
> 29 And straightway the fountain of her blood was dried
> up; and she felt in her body that she was healed of that
> plague.
> 30 And Jesus, immediately knowing in himself that
> VIRTUE [the Greek says "power"] had gone out of him,
> turned him about in the press, and said, Who touched my
> clothes?
> 31 And his disciples said unto him, Thou seest the multi-
> tude thronging thee, and sayest thou, Who touched me?
> 32 And he looked round about to see her that had done this
> thing.
> 33 But the woman fearing and trembling, knowing what
> was done in her, came and fell down before him, and told
> him all the truth.
> 34 And he said unto her, Daughter, thy faith hath made
> thee whole; go in peace, and be whole of thy plague.

When the woman touched Jesus, it says that "virtue"
went out of Him. Actually, the Greek word is always
translated "power" elsewhere. Power went out of Jesus
into her — there was a transfer of power.

What caused that power to go out of Him into her? Her
faith. He said, *"Daughter, thy faith hath made thee*

whole .... " (v. 34).

We see a similar passage in the 14th chapter of Matthew's Gospel:

> MATTHEW 14:34-36
> 34 And when they were gone over, they came into the land of Gennesaret.
> 35 And when the men of that place had knowledge of him, they sent out into all that country round about, and brought unto him all that were diseased;
> 36 And besought him THAT THEY MIGHT ONLY TOUCH THE HEM OF HIS GARMENT: and as many as touched were made perfectly whole.

Although this does not say that power went out of Jesus, it strongly infers it, because we know what happened in Mark 5.

Now let's look at Luke 6:

> LUKE 6:17-19
> 17 And he came down with them, and stood in the plain, and the company of his disciples, and a great multitude of people out of all Judea and Jerusalem, and from the sea coast of Tyre and Sidon, which came to hear him, and to be healed of their diseases;
> 18 And they that were vexed with unclean spirits: and they were healed.
> 19 And the whole multitude sought to touch him: for there went VIRTUE [or power] out of him, and healed them all.

This power that went out of Jesus not only healed the people of diseases, but the Bible says it healed people with unclean spirits. It was healing power. This sounds familiar to language used in the Acts of the Apostles:

> ACTS 19:11,12
> 11 And God wrought special miracles by the hands of Paul:

**12 So that from his body were brought unto the sick hand-
kerchiefs or aprons, and the diseases departed from them,
and the evil spirits went out of them.**

Here again we see people being healed of diseases and
being delivered from evil spirits. The Bible says in the
mouth of two or three witnesses shall every word be
established. We can learn something about this healing
power from these Scriptures.

First, we can be anointed with healing power as God
wills, but we can't anoint ourselves. (If we could, we'd all
be anointed.) God anoints some people to heal just like He
anoints others to preach, teach, and stand in various
offices.

Notice that we can't anoint one another. The Bible says,
"How *God anointed* Jesus of Nazareth" and "*God
wrought* special miracles by the hands of Paul.''

The healing anointing is the power of God. It's the
same Spirit; it's just a different anointing. It feels different.

The best way to describe it is to liken it to a coat. If
size 32 long fits you, you would be able to get into a size
40, but it wouldn't fit you exactly. You might even put
on a size 48, but it would look like an overcoat on you.

Sometimes when the anointing comes on me it feels as
if I'm wearing a coat — it's as if somebody threw an overcoat on me. Then, after I have ministered for a time, I've
felt it lift like a burden. It has seemed to fly away.

You can't continue to minister healing to the people
the same way after the anointing has lifted, so what do
you do?

I tell the people, "Well, praise God, the Bible's still so.
I won't lie to you — I can't minister with the anointing

anymore tonight, because the anointing has lifted. But I'll tell you what: Faith in God's Word *always* works. I was healed that way. I'll minister to you like that in faith if you want hands laid on you."

You can minister to people in faith without any anointing. I've seen people healed of incurable cancer and other conditions just sitting back there in the crowd. They believed the Word that was preached and believed God. They didn't particularly *feel* anything; they just released their faith. And, of course, God answered their faith.

Doctors predicted one such fellow would be dead in a month. It's been four years, and he's still alive. His doctors can't find a trace of cancer; he was healed by faith alone.

On the other hand, in the same services the Spirit of God has suddenly moved on me and I've done things I didn't even know I was doing. In ministering under that anointing you can get so far under you don't know what's happening around you, because you're moving over in the realm of the Spirit. I minister both ways, but right now we're studying about ministering with and under the anointing.

Second, this power is not only a heavenly materiality; it's a tangible substance. "Tangible" means perceptible to the touch, capable of being touched.

It has to be tangible, because Jesus knew the moment it flowed out of Him. He was aware of an outflow.

It has to be tangible, because the woman with the issue of blood was aware of receiving the power. There was a transmission of power from one to the other.

That woman did not touch Jesus' person, for He said, *"Who touched my clothes?"* His disciples replied, *"Thou seest the multitude thronging thee, and sayest thou, Who touched me?"* (Mark 5:31).

There's no telling how many people touched His clothes. We read in verse 27 that the woman had come "in the press behind." That means the people were pressing in on every side — pressing up against each other. Yet this power didn't flow out to all of them; it only flowed out to this woman.

Third, the healing power is transferable or transmittable: It will flow from one person to another, mainly by touch, such as by the laying on of hands. We saw in Luke 6:19 that "... *the whole multitude SOUGHT TO TOUCH HIM: for there went virtue* [or power] *out of him, and healed them all."*

How Healing Power Is 'Stored'

Another way the healing anointing is transmitted from one person to another is by the application of a cloth or handkerchief to a sick person's body. We need to realize that this healing power is capable of being "stored" in cloth, as it was in Jesus' garment and in the handkerchiefs of Paul, as we saw in Acts 19:12.

Evidently Jesus' clothes had absorbed that anointing, and it flowed out to the woman when she touched His robe. Evidently that's what happened with Paul when he laid his hands on those handkerchiefs. The anointing he was anointed with flowed into those cloths and they became "storage batteries," so to speak, of that anointing or power. Then, when the cloths were laid on the sick, the diseases departed from them, and evil spirits went out of them.

But God did it all: God anointed Jesus of Nazareth, and God wrought special miracles by the hands of Paul. Jesus said of His own ministry, "*...the Father that dwelleth in me, he doeth the works*" (John 14:10). That same power accomplished the same results in Paul's ministry when those cloths were laid on the sick.

We will elaborate a little on this point. Often, in our narrow thinking, we do not allow God to do everything He wants to do, because we imagine things have to be done in a certain way.

For example, many believe demons or devils always have to be discerned and cast out. The demons weren't discerned or cast out in the Scriptures we just studied, were they? Not in either case, yet the people were delivered. That just happens sometimes.

People have come up to me in the healing line and said, "I think maybe I have a demon."

I answer, "What difference does it make? The same power that will drive out sickness will drive out devils. That power went into you when I prayed. Forget it and go on faith; you're delivered."

That's the trouble — people go by what they think instead of by what the Bible says. Of course, if you're operating in faith without the healing anointing, then you do have to speak the Word, but it doesn't say anything about Jesus' speaking any Word at all in the sixth chapter of Luke: "*And they that were vexed with unclean spirits... were healed. And the whole multitude sought to touch him: for there went virtue* [power] *out of him, and healed them all*" (vv. 18,19). That means all those with diseases *and* evil spirits were healed.

In my own ministry, I've seen any number of alcoholics

healed, and I didn't know one of them was an alcoholic. In fact, some of them didn't even come up for prayer for their alcoholism; they came up for healing, because when you drink too much the alcohol affects your liver and you get ulcers. (There's no doubt in my mind at all that alcoholism is a demon.)

I've had any number of people tell me, "Brother Hagin, when you laid hands on me, that anointing came into me, and I was delivered from alcoholism."

One such testimony came from a man who had been an officer in the U.S. Army. He had been in three government hospitals and three private hospitals. "I took the cure for alcoholism," he told me, "and came out drinking."

He was a man nearly 60 years old. He said, "I remembered when I was 13 years old I knew the Lord. I knew the story of the Prodigal Son, so I got down on my knees and prayed, 'Dear Lord, I'm coming home, just like the Prodigal Son of old, and I ask You to forgive me.' "

He said, "I know the Lord took me back. I had peace in my spirit. It felt to me like a 2,000-pound weight rolled off my chest. But my body still was bound with that alcohol demon. I couldn't quit drinking."

A friend invited him to one of our meetings, and he went. He hadn't been to church in years, and he didn't understand what was happening in the service as people lifted their hands and prayed as one, right out loud.

The church he had gone to as a youngster was quiet and conservative. He told me later, "Then you started that healing line and nearly everybody you laid hands on fell on the floor, and that startled me. I said to my friend, 'Well, I'm going down there because I need help desperately, but I'm not going to fall like the rest of them!' "

He told me, "The next thing I knew, I was getting up off the floor. I don't even remember falling. Two outstanding things happened to me: First, when you laid hands on me, something like electricity went all over me — warmth went all over me. It was a great spiritual experience. I got closer to Jesus. It made me love Him more. Second, that alcohol demon I was bound with all those years left me. I've never touched another drop. I've never even *wanted* another drink!" Thank God for the power of God — the anointing.

Healed — And Delivered

People with all kinds of demon activity — people who had been mixed up with spiritualism and the occult — all kinds of demon manifestations — have been set free the same way after coming forward for healing. They didn't even have deliverance in mind.

One person said to me, "I came because I had stomach trouble and I wanted to get healed. I not only got healed, but since that power came into me, I've never heard another rapping on the wall in the nighttime. I've never heard any more voices. All that activity stopped."

Thank God, the diseases "departed from them, and the evil spirits went out of them." For there is a power that is greater than the power of the devil. There is a power that's greater than disease and sickness. It is the power of God.

How does this power operate? Jesus is anointed with it, but how are you going to get that anointing over to someone else?

The anointing will manifest in various ways. John G.

Lake compared it to electricity. He said, "Electricity is God's power in the natural realm, but the Holy Ghost power is God's power in the spirit realm."

Electricity flows, doesn't it? So there is a similarity, because this supernatural power also flows.

After men discovered electricity, they had to learn the rules and laws that governed it. They finally learned how to get electricity to flow. They learned that not just anything — not just any metal — will conduct electricity.

And I've learned from experience that not just any material or substance will conduct God's power. We have seen in Scripture that that anointing will flow right into cloth, as it did into Jesus' clothes and Paul's handkerchiefs.

Even though paper has some of the same ingredients in it, I never have been able to get that anointing to go into paper, leather, or any other substance. But it will flow into cloth. Why? I don't know. In the same way, I don't know why every kind of material or metal will not conduct electricity, but it won't.

We can say, however, that the Holy Spirit power *flowed* out of Jesus into the woman with the issue of blood. We could use a scriptural terminology and say that the Holy Spirit power *flows like water*, because Jesus Himself said:

JOHN 7:37-39
37 In the last day, that great day of the feast, Jesus stood and cried, saying, If any man thirst, let him come unto me, and drink. [When you think about thirst and drinking, you think about water.]
38 He that believeth on me, as the scripture hath said, out of his belly shall flow [out of his innermost being shall flow] rivers [that's water, isn't it?] of living water.

> 39 (But this spake he of the Spirit, which they that believe on him should receive: for the Holy Ghost was not yet given; because that Jesus was not yet glorified.)

Back then, Jesus couldn't have used the illustration of electricity because it wasn't known. People wouldn't have known what He was talking about. But they did know about water and about water flowing.

A Transferable Power

So the Holy Spirit flows like electricity or water. It will flow from one person to another. Therefore, this power — this healing power — is not only a tangible substance and a heavenly materiality; this power is transmittable or transferable.

It can be transmitted from one person to another, or transferred from one through another.

Evidently Jesus did that when He called His twelve disciples to Him and gave them power:

> MATTHEW 10:1
> 1   And when he had called unto him his twelve disciples, HE GAVE THEM POWER against unclean spirits, to cast them out, and to heal all manner of sickness and all manner of disease.

The Word of God says in John 3:34 that Jesus had the Spirit without measure, so when He sent forth the Twelve, He gave them power. Where did He get this power? We saw in Acts 10:38 that *"God anointed Jesus of Nazareth with the Holy Ghost and power."*

Often, even in ministry, something is transferred from one person to another. The Word of God says in the 34th chapter of Deuteronomy that Joshua had the same spirit of wisdom that Moses had, because Moses had laid his hands on him:

DEUTERONOMY 34:9
9 And Joshua the son of Nun was full of the spirit of wisdom; for Moses had laid his hands upon him . . . .

Evidently some of that same spiritual wisdom and power Moses was anointed with was transferred to Joshua by the laying on of hands, for the power of God is transferable.

In Luke 10:19, Jesus said to the Seventy: *"Behold, I give unto you power to tread on serpents and scorpions, and over all the power of the enemy: and nothing shall by any means hurt you."* I know the Greek word here is also translated "authority," but whether it's authority or literal power, Jesus is sending them out to do the same works He did: He healed the sick and cast out devils with the power of God.

Are His disciples going to do these things with human power? No, if they could do that, they'd already have been doing it.

Jesus authorized and evidently empowered His disciples to go out and heal and deliver people. In Mark 9, we see that in their journeys they ran into a fellow whom Jesus hadn't empowered, yet he was casting out devils by faith. They forbade him to do so, and came back and reported this to Jesus.

But Jesus said, *"Forbid him not: for there is no man which shall do a miracle in my name, that can lightly speak evil of me"* (Mark 9:39).

This fellow was casting out spirits in the Name of Jesus, and he didn't even know Him. He was a stranger to Jesus. Jesus didn't know him, and He hadn't called him. He hadn't said, "I authorize you. I give you power." This fellow had been in some of Jesus' services and he had faith to cast out devils. Notice he was casting them out through faith. When the disciples ministered, they did so with the anointing.

You can produce the same results by faith that you can with the anointing. There's no use being divided on the subject.

Some people who minister under the anointing know nothing about faith. That was one of the major problems we had in the days of the great Healing Revival here in the United States in 1947-58. Almost all of the healing evangelists were ministering under the anointing — the power of God — but some of them knew very little about the Bible. (They made some of the most stupid statements concerning the Bible you ever heard in your life.)

Most of the ministers involved in this movement belonged to the Voice of Healing organization. We always had a convention at Thanksgiving. At our 1954 convention in Philadelphia, I said to some of the brethren, "When all the rest of these fellows are gone, I'll still be out there ministering." They're all gone except one or two of us, and I'm still ministering.

Why? Because I saw the difference between ministering under an anointing and ministering by faith, and I minister both ways.

What happened to the others? Preacher after preacher got sick themselves. These were men who had been mightily used of God to do marvelous things, but they ministered only under the anointing. Some of them came to talk to me after they got sick.

One man said, "This anointing — this gift or whatever ministry I've got — will work for other people, but it won't work for me." (The anointing is always there to minister to somebody else.) "Why won't it work for me?" he asked.

I said, "God didn't give the ministry of the apostle to minister to the apostle. He gave it to minister to the Body of Christ. You're going to have to get healed like the rest of us — by faith — or else do without it." He looked at me like he'd seen a ghost.

"Well," he said, "I guess I'll do without it, because I don't know anything about faith."

I said, "You ought to have been listening when some of us who do know something about it were preaching and teaching. Just because you're anointed to do something doesn't mean you know everything."

I'm thinking of another fellow. One night they brought five adults from a school for the deaf and dumb to his service. All five were instantly healed. He laid his hands on a blind woman. Instantly her eyes were opened. Another person came in on a stretcher. Her doctor had given her up to die. She was instantly healed.

Yet the preacher didn't know a thing in the world about the Bible when it came to faith and very little when it came to healing. I nearly fell off my seat one night at one statement the poor fellow made. And then he got sick.

The anointing would come on him, he'd minister under it, some of the greatest things you've ever seen would happen, and then the anointing would lift.

The anointing doesn't remain on you in manifestation, because you'd wear out physically. You couldn't stand it. It's like getting hold of a live electric wire — you couldn't hold on to it forever.

I've had such a strong anointing on me that I've vibrated — I've shaken physically under it. Even my eyeballs jumped! I've had such a strong anointing on me that I couldn't even see the crowd. They thought I was looking right at them, but I didn't even know they were there, for I was over in this other realm.

I get more results when I get over there, but I don't stay over there, because I can't stand it. My body's still mortal, and I can't stand it.

I've had to say to the Lord, "Lord, turn it off! Just turn it off! I can't stand it. I can't take any more!"

Some time ago we were having dinner with friends in the ministry, and we were talking about the healing anointing.

This evangelist said, "Through the years, I've always woven in and out of the healing anointing — I haven't always had that anointing on me — but in recent times it has come back on me.

"Sometimes I'm sitting here in the living room at night, talking to my wife, and when I get up to go to bed and step into the bedroom, it's as if I've stepped into a room full of glory. It's just all over me. I can hardly stand it. It's the anointing — the healing anointing. I have to say, 'Lord, turn it off. I can't take any more.' "

I know exactly what he's talking about. Physically, you just can't take it. Jesus had the Holy Spirit without measure. If I get a little too much measure of it, I can't stand it.

The Spirit Without Measure

The reason Jesus could have the Spirit without measure is because His body was not mortal.

Yes, He could be tempted in all points like we are, because He was human, all right, but He was like Adam was before he sinned. Adam could be tempted — but before Adam sinned, his body was neither mortal nor immortal. (On the other hand, Adam did need to sustain that human body by eating.)

If Adam's body had been mortal, it would have been subject to death — but *Adam originally wasn't subject to death.* The Word of God says that death affects you when you sin: *"Wherefore, as by one man sin entered into the world, and death by sin; so death passed upon all men, for that all have sinned"* (Rom. 5:12). Death didn't pass on mankind until after Adam had sinned.

This is the reason Jesus couldn't be killed until He was made sin for us. Jesus said, *"No man taketh it* [His life] *from me, but I lay it down of myself"* (John 10:18).

Once an angry mob was going to throw Him off the brow of a hill at Nazareth to kill Him, but He slipped through their midst and disappeared (Luke 4:29,30).

Then, in the Garden of Gethsemane, when He took upon His spirit nature our sins and our diseases, His body became mortal, and they could kill Him.

But in all His earthly ministry, Jesus had the Holy Spirit without measure. Just imagine: Jesus had the Spirit without measure, and it could flow through Him and not particularly bother or affect Him!

Let's go back to the illustration Dr. Lake gave that electricity is God's power in the natural realm. Physically, you can take a little electric shock and sometimes a little static electricity. You feel it and shake it off. It doesn't affect your body. But if you grab hold of a lamp that's got a short in it and that power hits you, you jump and holler! You can't stand there all day holding on to that lamp. In fact, even 110 volts will kill you under certain circumstances. And if you move up to higher voltage, it will fry your hide!

I can stand only so much anointing, and I can't stand it for very long. There are times I feel as if I'm going to fall down — it seems my legs are going out from under me. My hands tingle. My arms tingle. Sometimes my whole body tingles. Sometimes the anointing in the palms of my hands burns like fire.

When the Lord appeared to me in that first vision on September 2, 1950 in that tent meeting in Rockwall, Texas, He touched the palms of my hands with the finger of His right hand, and my hands began to burn as if I were holding a coal of fire in them. It wasn't just a warmth — they felt as if they were burning.

For three days and nights my hands burned until I'd catch myself rubbing them, trying to get a little relief.

The thing that was special about this anointing was the added dimension. It's the same anointing, except a different measure. It's the same Holy Spirit — there's only one Holy Spirit. (There are a lot of spirits in the world, but they are demon spirits. We're not interested in them, and we're not afraid of them, because we have authority over them.)

Jesus said, "If that leaves you, fast and pray until it comes back." So *if the anointing wanes, I'll do a little fasting and a little extra praying, and it will come back in force.*

A Special Anointing

He said, "Kneel before me," and I knelt before Him.

He laid His hand on my head and said, "I've called thee and have anointed thee and have given unto thee a special anointing to minister to the sick." Then He said, "Stand upright on thy feet. You understand this is not the only way to minister healing to the sick."

I replied, "I know that. I've been doing it differently for years." And we talked about the different ways.

Then He said, "This anointing will not work unless you tell the people exactly what I told you."

Why would He want me to say that? There is a principle here. We saw it in the story of the woman with the issue of blood. Notice what Jesus said to her: *"Daughter, thy faith hath made thee whole."* Faith has something to do with healing.

Some will say, "Well, I thought it was that anointing — that power — that went out of Him that healed her." Yes, that's sometimes true, but *it's your faith that makes you whole.*

How did the woman get faith? Why would she have faith in Him or in the anointing He was anointed with? In Mark 5:27,28 it says, *"When SHE HAD HEARD OF JESUS . . .* [she] *came in the press behind, and touched his garment, For she said, If I may touch but his clothes, I shall be whole."*

Jesus told me, "This will not work for you unless you TELL the people exactly what I told you." Why does He want me to tell you? So you can believe it.

He said, "Tell the people exactly what I told you. That is, you tell them you saw me. Tell them I spoke to you. Tell them I laid the finger of my right hand in the palm of each one of your hands. Tell them the healing anointing is in your hands."

Jesus' Sense of Humor

Then He smiled — I can see Him yet, how He smiled — and said, talking about the anointing in my hands, "The anointing is not in your feet — I didn't tell you to lay your feet on anybody. The anointing is not in your head — I didn't tell you to lay your head on anybody. It's in your hands." And He grinned when He said that. I believe He has a sense of humor, don't you? (I know so.)

"Tell them that I told you to tell them that if they will believe that — that is, believe that you're anointed — and will receive the anointing, that power will flow from your hands into their body and will drive out their sickness or their disease, or will effect a healing or a cure in them. " (Notice He called it "that power" this time instead of calling it the anointing.)

I began to minister with that anointing. In January 1952, I was holding a meeting in Port Arthur, Texas. In those days, after I'd preached and given the altar call, I'd send people to the prayer room to be saved and I'd put others in a prayer line to be healed and filled with the Holy Spirit. I'd sit on a chair on the platform and lay hands on them as they went by. I'd spend time with each of them, talking to them individually. We had 25 to 50 people a night in the prayer lines in those days, so we could take the time to do this.

One night I was sitting in the chair ministering when suddenly a stronger anointing came on me. One can be more or less anointed to minister healing, preach, or stand in any office. We're talking about *ministering* here.

The Personal Anointing

Every born-again, Spirit-filled believer has a measure

of the Spirit and anointing within, John 2:27 says, but this "personal anointing" never will be increased. There's nothing in the Scripture that indicates you can have a double portion of your personal anointing.

Yes, Elisha had a double portion of what Elijah had, but that was *an anointing to minister.*

As I was sitting in that chair, it felt as if somebody threw something over me. I could feel it in my whole being — it was as if someone had thrown a cloak over my shoulders. It was vibrating through every part of me — I knew it in my spirit. I also knew it wouldn't last long, because I couldn't physically stand it that long, so I leaped off the platform and ran by the people in the healing line, touching them on the forehead as I ran by.

I was so overwhelmed by the Spirit that the pastor had to tell me later what I had done. I remembered starting to run, but I couldn't see anything, even though I had my eyes wide open. (It's difficult to describe spiritual things.)

The Ordinary Anointing

Everyone I touched fell under the power (that had only happened once or twice to me as a pastor). Suddenly that anointing lifted from me. I looked around and saw all those people lying on the floor. I returned to the platform, sat down, and finished the healing line with what I call the "ordinary anointing."

Later the pastor told me I had laid hands on 34 people. He said, "About 17 of them had come to get the Holy Spirit, and they were lying there on the floor talking in tongues. Most of them are members of my church. That astounds me — I've never seen anything like it — because some of them were chronic seekers; they'd been seeking the baptism of the Holy Spirit for years."

That didn't happen again until September 1954, when I preached the three Sunday services in the First Foursquare Church of San Jose, California.

At the close of the morning service, I dismissed the people and said, "You come back this afternoon and we'll lay hands on believers to be filled with the Holy Spirit and we'll lay hands on the sick to be healed."

That afternoon we had the people who wanted to be filled with the Spirit to stand on one side and those who wanted healing to stand in another line. The pastor and a minister friend were ministering with me. Just as I started down the line, the anointing came on me. Again, it was as if somebody had run by me and had thrown a cloak on me. I could feel it all over me. Again, I knew it wouldn't last long because I could not physically stand it, so I started running and touching people with my finger. (I didn't take time to touch them with my hands.)

I was caught up in that glory, and they told me everybody I touched fell. Then that anointing lifted from me. I couldn't have stood it any longer.

That stronger anointing has come on me four times in the past 20 years.

In September 1970, while my wife and I were in New York State, the Lord instructed me to return to Tulsa and hold a seminar. Our offices then were in Brother T. L. Osborn's old office building on North Utica. We had a little chapel in there that would seat 300, so we'd hold a seminar now and then.

The Lord told me to have a Healing Seminar at night and a Prayer Seminar in the mornings from October 11-18,

1970. He said, "Teach on intercessory prayer." (Those messages were later made into the book *The Interceding Christian*.)

'That Stronger Anointing'

He told me what to teach on in every service. "When you come to Wednesday night," He said, "speak on special ministries and special anointings. Relate your experience of what I said to you 20 years ago when I appeared to you, and then lay hands on the people.

"And when you lay hands on them, that stronger anointing that has come on you four times in the last 20 years will come to abide. This will be a new beginning for you. You see, you've never done what you should have done with the healing ministry."

(I've been running ever since then, trying to keep up with what God's doing. It takes all my time and effort to try to keep up with Him!)

Six weeks before that 1970 seminar I had a vision of people lying all over the front of that little auditorium and up on the platform. I knew what was going to happen, but I didn't tell a soul. I didn't want to be accused of causing it or influencing it somehow.

When I started laying hands on the people during that seminar, they started falling everywhere. The anointing on me was strong.

After ministering that night, I wobbled around like a drunk. I couldn't get to my car unaided, much less drive it home. Somebody had to drive me home and help me out of the car. They got me in a big recliner, but it was two hours before I got back to normal and could get up out of the chair and walk.

This is one reason I get away from the crowd in healing crusades. The anointing seems to settle down in my legs like that and I can't walk.

Also, when I'm ministering under that anointing, I'll tell people, "Don't talk to me." You see, if I get back over in the natural, mental realm, I'll lose the anointing. So I don't want people to touch me or do anything that would bring me back into the physical realm. I want to be left alone.

My wife and the people who work with me in the crusades tell me things that happen in the healing line that I never know happened (that doesn't mean I'm unconscious). Sometimes funny things happen, and they'll start laughing, but if I were to be aware of it and laugh with them, I'd lose the anointing and would get back over into the natural.

I always have a measure of that anointing — always. And I can begin talking about it and it will come into manifestation to a lesser or greater degree. Often the palms of both my hands will start burning.

Making the Anointing Stronger

I can make the anointing come on me stronger by doing certain things: a little fasting, a little extra prayer, a little extra waiting on God, although I don't always have time to do that.

This brings me to another thought: *I have found that when I have a stronger anointing, I always have more instant healings.*

I've had great success in the past, and still do, ministering to people with cancer, but only a few persons over a period of years were instantly healed.

Even though that power will flow into people and they receive it, their healing doesn't always happen instantly. Sometimes it would be three to ten days before they could tell a difference — but that power drove the cancer out of their bodies.

Most healing is by degree, based on two conditions:

(1) *The degree of healing virtue administered;*

(2) *The degree of faith that gives action to the power administered.*

It doesn't matter how strongly I'm anointed — if there's not faith to give action to that power, there'll be no healing. We can prove this by looking at Proverbs 4:

PROVERBS 4:20-22

20 My son, attend to my words; incline thine ear unto my sayings.
21 Let them not depart from thine eyes; keep them in the midst of thine heart.
22 For they are life unto those that find them, and health to all their flesh.

If you've got a good reference Bible, you will notice a little number or letter by the word "health." The marginal note will indicate that in the original Hebrew, the word translated "health" was originally the word "medicine." In other words, God is saying, "my words are medicine to all their flesh."

Do you know any medicine that will cure you after just one dose? No, nobody does. You're not going to take just one dose of the Word and be well, either. I know it said He sent His Word and healed them, but He said "my words are medicine."

Exploring the Realm of the Spirit

Ever since the first night that anointing came on me to abide, as Jesus had promised, the potential has been there all the time. But I've never had the anointing that strong again in these past 13 years. It's been close a time or two, but it took me two hours to get back to the natural that time.

I don't know if you've had any experience in the Spirit or not, but I've had a lot of experience, and I'll be perfectly honest with you: When that anointing comes, you almost get afraid from the natural standpoint, because you're afraid you can't get back.

In August 1982, the anointing came on me so strong out at Fred Price's church, Crenshaw Christian Center, in Inglewood, California, that I couldn't say a word in English, and I couldn't get back. I kept thinking during that experience, *I'm not going to get back. I'm so far out, I can't get back!*

"What do you mean 'get back'?" some will ask.

I know exactly what happened to Enoch. He got out in the realm of the Spirit, and he couldn't get back. I want to get back, so I don't get out too far.

We are exploring today in the realm of the Spirit, learning some things we should have known yesterday.

In modern times, men have explored outer space. But they didn't get to the moon the first time; they barely got out of the hold of gravity and over into that other realm at first.

Why? Because they didn't know what was out there. They didn't know the rules and laws that regulate space. They didn't know if they could get back or not! So they barely went out at first, looked around, and then went a

little farther and a little farther each time. Finally they
went all the way to the moon and walked on it.

I think there's a parallel here, because Daniel, years
ago, prophesied about these last days. He said, *"Many
shall run to and fro, and knowledge shall be increased"*
(Dan. 12:4).

Knowledge *has* been increased. Some of us have been
out there a little on the edge of the Spirit, but we don't
get out too far.

(People get baptized with the Holy Spirit, speak with
tongues, and think *This is it!* No, this isn't it. No, no, no!)

There are spacemen and now spacewomen. We're going
to be doing exploits out here in the Spirit, while they're
doing exploits out there in space.

From this place — RHEMA Bible Training Center —
we're going to send out "Spiritmen" and "Spiritwomen."

SECTION III
The Corporate Anointing

Chapter 15
The Corporate Anointing

I'm thoroughly convinced — although you can neither prove nor disprove it by the Bible — that we as the Body of Christ *as a whole* have *the same measure* of the Holy Spirit that Jesus did — but we as individual members of the Body of Christ do not.

The greatest anointing of all is the corporate anointing.

Let's look at some Scriptures in the Old Testament. The Old Testament is full of types and shadows for us.

In Second Chronicles 5 we learn how the Temple of God was dedicated.

> 2 CHRONICLES 5:11-14
> 11 And it came to pass, when the priests were come out of the holy place: (for all the priests that were present were sanctified, and did not then wait by course:
> 12 Also the Levites which were the singers, all of them of Asaph, of Heman, of Jeduthun, with their sons and their brethren, being arrayed in white linen, having cymbals and psalteries and harps, stood at the east end of the altar, and with them an hundred and twenty priests sounding with trumpets:)
> 13 It came even to pass, as the trumpeters and singers were as one, to make one sound to be heard in praising and thanking the Lord; and when they lifted up their voice with the trumpets and cymbals and instruments of musick, and praised the Lord, saying, For he is good; for his mercy endureth for ever: that then the house was filled with a cloud, even the house of the Lord;
> 14 So that the priests could not stand to minister by reason of the cloud: for the glory of the Lord had filled the house of God.

When the Temple was dedicated, the building was filled with a literal cloud. That cloud was the glory of God.

All through the Old Testament, the glory of God appeared often as a cloud and filled the house. We read from the New Testament that the glory of God is the Spirit of God.

Romans 6 tells us Christ was raised up from the dead by the glory of the Father. Romans 8:11 tells us, *"But if the Spirit of him that raised up Jesus from the dead dwell in you . . . ."* It says He was raised up by the glory of the Father. The Bible calls the glory of the Father the Spirit — so that's the Holy Spirit. We call it the anointing.

Jesus said, *"The Spirit of the Lord is upon me, because he hath anointed me . . . ."* (Luke 4:18).

The Temple of God in the Old Testament was a man-made building. But God no longer dwells in earth-made or man-made buildings; He dwells in us.

Hebrews 3:6 tells us the difference between the house of God in the Old Testament and the house of God in the New Testament: *"But Christ as a son over his own house; whose house are we, if we hold fast the confidence and the rejoicing of the hope firm unto the end."*

The whole Church collectively is God's temple.

Now notice First Timothy 3:15: *"But if I tarry long, that thou mayest know how thou oughtest to behave thyself in the house of God, which is the church of the living God, the pillar and ground of truth."*

He's not talking about a building; he's talking about the Church. The Church of the Living God is the house of God.

First Corinthians 3:16 says, *"Know ye not that ye are the temple of God, and that the Spirit of God dwelleth in you?"* In the Old Testament, Solomon's Temple was called the house of God three times. But now we are the house of God. *The Amplified Bible* says, "Do you not discern and understand that you [the whole church at Corinth] are God's temple (His sanctuary), and that God's Spirit has His permanent dwelling in you — to be at home in you [collectively as a church and also individually]?" (1 Cor. 3:16).

So you can see there is the individual anointing within us because that Spirit — that anointing — is in us, but then there's also that *corporate* anointing. We're conscious of His presence in our midst so many times. But why doesn't He manifest Himself more often?

Let's go back to the Old Testament and see what was done to bring forth the visible manifestation of God's glory.

Second Chronicles 5:13 tells us of singers and those playing instruments becoming as one singing praises unto God, saying, *"For he is good; for his mercy endureth for ever."* Then the cloud came in and filled the building so the priests could not stand to minister.

There's something about that corporate body praising God that brings forth the manifestation of His glory. The Pentecostals saw it earlier, but modern-day charismatics don't know too much about it.

Oh yes, we praise God and clap our hands, and that's scriptural; but God wants to teach us something about His Spirit so we'll enter into the full manifestation of what He has for us. For the corporate anointing is much greater than the individual anointing.

Let's look at some Scriptures in the New Testament that will parallel the Old Testament Scriptures and will help us.

> **ACTS 2:46,47**
> **46 And they, continuing daily with one accord in the temple, and breaking bread from house to house, did eat their meat with gladness and singleness of heart,**
> **47 Praising God, and having favour with all the people. And the Lord added to the church daily such as should be saved.**

There are three things to note about these two verses of Scripture: first, "one accord"; second, "gladness"; and third, "praising God."

In Acts 4 Peter and John were commanded to preach and teach no more.

> **ACTS 4:23,24**
> **23 And being let go, they went to their own company, and reported all that the chief priests and elders had said unto them.**
> **24 And when they heard that, they lifted up their voice to God with ONE ACCORD, and said, Lord, thou art God, which hast made heaven, and earth, and the sea, and all that in them is.**

There's that "one accord" business again. They (plural) — all of them — lifted up their voices. We have a record of the prayer they prayed. I know they didn't all say the same words, but the Holy Spirit is inspiring Luke to write, and He is giving us what God heard.

The Effects of Praise

Notice when they lifted up their voices with one accord, the first thing they said was, *"Lord, thou art God"* (v. 24). They were magnifying Him as God. And when they had prayed, the place was shaken. That prayer brought forth a manifestation of God's glory, of God's power, of the anointing, of the Holy Spirit power. The *place* was shaken — not just the people. The house shook.

Some people get excited because the Holy Spirit moves on people and they shake sometimes, or even fall under the power. But wait until the buildings start shaking! The place was shaken where they were assembled together, and they were all filled with the Holy Spirit and spoke the Word of God with boldness.

In the 16th chapter of Acts, Paul and Silas had been beaten. Their backs were bleeding. They were thrust into the innermost prison. Their feet were in stocks. And at midnight, Paul and Silas prayed.

A lot of times people have prayed and prayed and prayed — and I've seen people go down praying. But sometimes you need to *"pray AND...."*

Paul and Silas didn't just pray; they prayed *AND*. They prayed *AND* sang praises unto God. They were doing it out loud, because all the prisoners heard them. Remember in Psalm 22:3 it says that God inhabits the praises of Israel. He's the same God now that He was then. He hasn't changed one iota.

God came down and inhabited the praises of Paul and Silas, and shook that old jail until every door flew open and the stocks fell off their feet. Acts 16:26 tells us, *"And suddenly there was a great earthquake, so that the foundations of the prison were shaken: and immediately all the doors were opened, and every one's bands were loosed."* But this wasn't an earthquake as we know it, because it just affected this one group. An earthquake wouldn't cause the bands the prisoners were bound with to fall off. It wouldn't cause the stocks on their feet to fall off. But the bands and stocks fell off them. Remember Isaiah 10:27 tells us the anointing breaks the yoke.

The Power of the Corporate Anointing

I can be anointed myself and lay hands on people, and a certain percentage of them will get healed. But the corporate anointing has a greater effect.

One time I was preaching and it seemed like a wind went through the building. Everybody heard it. And that fast, every sinner in the building was saved. Every backslider was reclaimed. Everyone who didn't have the Holy Spirit sat there talking in tongues. Every sick person was healed.

There was a woman who was lying on a stretcher. She had been operated on six times and doctors had said there was no use operating anymore. She'd been given six months to live and four of those months were gone. She looked like the picture of death — just a corpse, wasted away. Nobody had prayed for her or touched her at the meeting, but when that wind went through, she leaped off the stretcher and ran up the aisles healed.

There was another woman who thought she was saved because she was a church member. But when the wind blew through she got saved — she realized she never had been saved before. She sat there talking in tongues. When she got home, all her physical ailments had disappeared. I was back in that place holding a revival later and she said, "Not only that, but I've never touched another cigarette; I have never even wanted one. The thought never occurred to me to smoke."

God wants us to have the greater corporate anointing

in these days, and we're going to have it. We're not a half step away from it.

In one of our Holy Spirit seminars at RHEMA Bible Training Center, I began to teach about the Holy Spirit within you in the New Birth, and the Holy Spirit upon you in the baptism with the Holy Spirit. One night as we all began to flow in the Spirit, the power of God fell on us and all 3,000 people were dancing. We had an African ambassador to the United Nations there, and even he was dancing in the Spirit.

Years ago in Pentecost I saw people dance in the Spirit — I dance in the Spirit myself sometimes — but I never saw anything like that in my life. We didn't have anything worked up, either. Too many times people try to work up something in the flesh. That doesn't produce any power. It's really obnoxious, in fact.

While we were dancing and praising God, people started getting healed all over the place. Just like you'd snapped your finger, people all over that building were healed as that corporate anointing began to work.

There was a 12-year-old boy there on crutches. He had broken his leg playing football. He laid down his crutches and came running down the aisle. He and my grandson stood on the platform weeping, and he was instantly healed. I didn't have to pray for anybody's healing. You see, we had become one in worship.

The Word of God says to praise God in the dance. Music and dancing belong to God and His people. The devil has stolen both and perverted them.

Did you ever notice the place praise had in the Old Testament? Some will argue, "Yes, but Brother Hagin, that's in the Old Testament."

I know it. That's just what I wanted you to say.

If praise had such a great place in worship and ministry in the Old Testament when they were operating under the type and shadow of the New, how much more of a place should it have with us?

United Prayer

Let's look at another New Testament example of united praying. Acts 13 tells us:

ACTS 13:1,2
1 Now there were in the church that was at Antioch certain prophets and teachers; as Barnabas, and Simeon that was called Niger, and Lucius of Cyrene, and Manaen, which had been brought up with Herod the tetrarch, and Saul.
2 As they ministered to the Lord, and fasted, the Holy Ghost said, Separate me Barnabas and Saul for the work whereunto I have called them.

These five men of God ministered to the Lord, and fasted, and it brought a manifestation of the Spirit; *it brought forth a revelation.*

If we can find out how they prayed, and if we'll pray the same way, it'll produce the same results.

Before we answer that, let's look also at the 22nd chapter of Acts: *"And it came to pass, that, when I was come again to Jerusalem, even while I prayed in the temple, I was in a trance"* (Acts 22:17). Paul was praying here and was in a trance. His praying brought forth a manifestation of God's power of the Holy Spirit. Jesus appeared to him and spoke to him: *"...Make haste, and get thee quickly out of Jerusalem: for they will not receive thy testimony concerning me"* (Acts 22:18).

How did Paul pray? I'm sure he prayed in his own language, but he gave us a little clue in First Corinthians 14:18 when he said, *"I thank my God, I speak with tongues more than ye all."*

In writing to the Church at Ephesus, he said, *"Praying always with all prayer and supplication in the Spirit, and watching thereunto with all perseverance and supplication for all saints"* (Eph. 6:18).

Remember, we looked at Acts 4:23,24. I'm sure some of those people were praying with their own understanding, but I'm sure that many of them were praying with their spirits. What we are told about is the interpretation of their voice. Did you notice they lifted up their "voice," not "voices"? I'm sure many of them were praying with other tongues. Paul, when he was praying in the Temple and fell into the trance, prayed in the Spirit as well as with his understanding (1 Cor. 14:14,15). It takes Spirit praying to produce Spirit results.

In Acts 13 when Paul and the others were ministering to the Lord, how do you suppose they did that? They did it in prayer and praise, or in song. Ephesians 5:19 tells us, *"Speaking to yourselves in psalms and hymns and spiritual songs, singing and making melody in your heart to the Lord."* That's ministering to the Lord, isn't it?

Let's go a step further. Paul, writing to the Church at Colosse, said, *"Let the word of Christ dwell in you richly in all wisdom; teaching and admonishing one another in psalms and hymns and spiritual songs, singing with grace in your hearts to the Lord"* (Col. 3:16). He said, "Singing to the Lord." Do you see that? We can minister not only to each other, but we can minister to the Lord. I'm sure that's what they were doing. They were speaking in psalms and hymns, and singing to the Lord, ministering to the Lord, praying in their own language and praying in tongues. And as they ministered to the Lord and fasted, the Holy Spirit spoke. You see, that kind of praying brings forth the manifestation of God's power and God's Spirit.

As these five ministered to the Lord and fasted, they were praying together. They were worshipping God together. There is something about united prayer; there's something about united praise; there's something about worshipping God in unity. I think the Lord knew what He was doing when He sent the disciples out two by two.

Jesus Himself made the statement in Matthew 18:19, *"...That if two of you shall agree on earth as touching any thing that they shall ask, it shall be done for them of my Father which is in heaven."*

Believers' Meetings

In the 12 years that I pastored, I was only able to bring one church to the place of unity that I feel the New Testament Church should be. It was an ordinary thing for miracles to happen. The supernatural was in manifestation. In those days, 1939 and 1940, we were in the tail end of the Depression. Things were different then. Our big crowds in those days were on Sunday nights.

You see, in 1939 you could go to the show if you had a dime. But nobody had a dime! So the sinners would come to church. They would fill up the building and the church yard. We didn't have air-conditioning, and in the spring, summer, and fall the windows were open. There were more people outside than inside. They would be standing 12 to 15 deep, all looking in. Out in front, all the way back to the street, they would be standing solid, looking in.

On Sunday mornings I had a different type of service than I did Sunday nights. The congregation was made up mostly of church members, so instead of an evangelistic service I'd have what I would call a "believers' meeting." Most of that time, over a couple of years, I didn't preach. I would just sit down on the platform and say, "I'm going to turn this over to the Holy Spirit. Whatever you've got, just get up and give it."

I would tell the people, "If you want to sing, if you want to dance, if you want to prophesy and speak with tongues, don't be afraid you'll get it wrong, because we'll straighten you out! We'll help you, not criticize you, but help you in love."

You know, we had some of the greatest moves you've ever seen in your life. Sometimes we'd sing and praise God; then we'd grow quiet. Those meetings would last sometimes until 1:30 or 2 o'clock in the afternoon. There were times we sat there from 45 minutes to an hour and a half — and nobody moved. We didn't have nurseries or Sunday School rooms, and we didn't even have any restrooms in the building.

But I've seen the power of God come in — the Holy Spirit come into His temple — the anointing come in — and there was a holy awe. That doesn't mean a fear like you would be afraid of a rattlesnake or a tornado. But that holy awe would come upon us. Nobody would say a word. Not a child would cry. You could have heard a pin drop. It seemed like you were afraid to move. The glory came in. It seemed like you could have cut a chunk out and taken it home with you.

There was one fellow who was unsaved and he would

bring his wife to Sunday School and church. Then he'd leave and go off uptown. He'd come back around noon to get her. But one day he drove onto the parking lot next to the church and couldn't hear anything. He got out of his car and came up to the window.

Later he said, "I knew everyone was in there because all the cars were on the parking lot. But I thought, *Did the Rapture take place?*"

He fully expected to look in and find the church empty. But he looked in and everyone was sitting there. He slipped in and sat on a back pew. We sat there ten more minutes and no one said anything. Suddenly, just sitting there, he started shaking. Then he got up and came down the aisle, shaking all over. He fell across the altar and cried out to God.

Nobody went to the altar to pray with him. We all just sat there. I said, "God started it; let Him finish it." That's our problem: We get in His way a lot of times.

My youngest brother, just 16 or 17 years old, came to visit one time in the summer. Through courtesy, he'd come to the services. He came to one of these believers' meetings. Suddenly, sitting in his chair, he started shaking. He got up and shook all the way down to the altar. He got saved and got up talking in tongues. We just let him go — we didn't even pray with him. God started it, so we let Him finish it.

I saw that happen many times. If a sinner happened to come in, 99 times out of 100 he would get saved without anyone saying a word to him. We ought to have the Holy Spirit in manifestation like that. They did years ago in the Methodist church. In Charles Finney's meetings the power of God would get on sinners and they would fall.

The miraculous — the supernatural — arrests people's attention. But I never could get most of the churches I pastored to that place of unity — to that place of flowing in the Spirit — to that place of praising God.

I believe God wants us to get back to that. I'm looking forward to meetings on a larger scale — like Campmeeting in Tulsa where we've got 20,000 people present — where the power of God will sweep through and we won't have to have any healing lines. Everybody will just go home healed. Everybody who doesn't have the Holy Spirit will go home talking in tongues. Everybody who's not saved will go home saved because of His power and presence.

I got back in Tulsa after holding some meetings in Denver one time, and a woman wrote me and said, "Brother Hagin, my husband and I want to give you a good report. I got my husband to come to one of your meetings. He wasn't saved, and he had a severe heart condition. Heart specialists said at best he could only live another six months."

She wanted to get him healed. She loved her husband. And she said, "I kept nagging on it; I kept harping on it. I finally got him to come. By the time we got there the building was full. Going up to the balcony was hard on his heart, but we finally got up there and we got the last two seats.

"I was so embarrassed. He'd talk right out loud while you were preaching and say, 'I don't believe a word of it. There's nothing to it.' People around him were telling him to be quiet. I was so embarrassed; I'd duck my head. At times he'd almost cuss; he used awful language.

"Then you started laying hands on people and they started falling under the power. He said, 'Nothing but hypnotism. That's all in the world it is.' "

Now, here's what she didn't know. I'm going to tell you my side of the story. I was laying hands on people in the healing line, and I saw the glory cloud roll in. It's like waves of the sea, but it's a cloud. I saw it coming, and I stepped back on the platform, because if I'd gotten in it, I would have gone down with everyone else. It came right over their heads, and when it did, I just waved my hand and they all went down like dominoes.

Now, this woman said, "You got down about halfway in that second healing line and suddenly you stepped back. (That was when I stepped back on the platform.) My husband said, 'It's going all over me; it's going all over me; it's going all over me!' "

She added, "I said to him, 'What's going all over you?' He said, 'That power you're talking about.' " And he was instantly healed.

She added, "I want you to know something. He's not only got a new physical heart, he's got a new spiritual heart. He's a new man!"

I believe that can happen in more than just a few isolated incidents. The glory can be in manifestation. This woman said her husband went back to the heart specialist and he said, "I'll tell you — Somebody up there likes you. You've got a brand new heart."

His heart was working perfectly. The glory of God had filled the temple of God.

You are the temple of God. Do you not discern and understand that the whole Church at Corinth — the whole Church here or wherever — YOU — are the temple of God? And that God's Spirit dwells in you collectively as the Church, and also individually?

We ought to expect Him to come into manifestation.
We expect Him to do what He said He would do — teach
us and lead us. We expect the minister to be anointed, and
we gripe if he's not, don't we? But what about our respon-
sibilities as members of that house of God — that Body
of God?

Prophecy

We're moving up now into the things of God!
And I heard the Spirit say,
There will come further revelation along these lines,
but it has to come line upon line,
precept upon precept.
And as it comes,
men and women will flow with the Spirit,
and there will be such a manifestation of
My power and My glory and My Spirit and My anointing
in these days — in this decade in which you live —
that it will startle men.
Now many who are on the fringes of the move of God
will draw back and say,
"Ahhh, that's fanaticism. No, we can't go with that.
We believe in doing things in a nice, sedate manner."
Never, never, never feel resentment
toward others who may criticize you,
or who may speak against you.
Never allow the least bit of resentment
or ill will, or bad feelings, but walk on.
Walk on in love.
Walk on in power.
Walk on in the Spirit.

Walk on with the Lord,
and He'll come unto thee and
manifest Himself unto thee.
And it is even written in
the Holy Scriptures
that His coming unto us
shall be as the rain.
And so the Holy Ghost will fall,
and the power of God will be in
manifestation, and great shall
be the reward thereof.
And many shall be blessed,
and great and good days stand just ahead.
Walk on. Yea, ye shall see,
for the glory of the Lord
shall appear unto thee.
But most will move with the Spirit,
and all will acknowledge,
"There are miracles happening over there.
I guess God just saw fit to have mercy on them."
But no, they saw fit to flow with God.
And they saw fit to go with God,
for He is at work in the earth tonight
and He indwells His Body which is the Church,
which is the house of God.
And His glory will fill that temple.
Many will say,
"I just don't go along with those things.
We have a pretty good church here.
God has put His approval upon us."
But yea, saith the Lord of Hosts,
I only put my approval upon

that which lines up with my Word.
Get into the Word
and let the Spirit open the Word to you.
Not only unto your mind,
but get the revelation of it in your spirit.
And your spirit will be more alive
unto the things of God.
And He — through your spirit — will be able
to teach you, and admonish you, and direct you.

Dr. Kenneth E. Hagin